Ruth Ogden

His little Royal Highness

Ruth Ogden

His little Royal Highness

ISBN/EAN: 9783337039783

Printed in Europe, USA, Canada, Australia, Japan

Cover: Foto ©ninafisch / pixelio.de

More available books at **www.hansebooks.com**

His Little Royal Highness

by
RUTH OGDEN

Author of "A Loyal Little Red-Coat."

Illustrated by
W. RAINEY.

New-York:
E. P. DUTTON & COMPANY.
31 West Twenty Third Street.
Printed in Bavaria.

CONTENTS.

Coronation Day	7
An Interview with Sister Julia	15
The Fairfaxes call on the Murrays	21
A Surprise for the Body-guard	28
Good-night and Good-bye	36
In the Highland Light.	41
A Trip to Burchard's	52
On the Way Home	61
A Day on the Beach	72
A Land Breeze	84
A New Friend	96
The "Starling" Runs Ashore	102
The Wreck of the Spanish Brig	111
A Puzzling Question	121
The Question Answered	127
The Captain's Story	138
Thanksgiving in Earnest	150
The King's Camera	155
Holidays in Town	170
In Mr. Vale's Church	178
In Mr. Vale's Study	184

"OH, blessed little kings and queens,
  The only sovereigns on the earth!
Their sovereignty nor rests nor leans
  On pomp of riches or of birth

No fortress built in all the land
  So strong they cannot storm it free.
No palace made too rich, too grand,
  For them to roam triumphantly.

THE only sovereigns on the earth
  Whose sway is certain to endure:
No line of kings of kingliest birth
  Is of its reigning half so sure"

"H. H"

I.

♔ Coronation Day

THE king's body-guard waited in the outer court of the palace, but the palace was only a dull, red cottage, and the court a low porch that surrounded three sides of it. As for the body-guard, they were not dressed as such great people are wont to be. One of them wore a calico dress, canvas shoes, and an untrimmed hat of soft red felt. The other, for there were but two of them, was resplendent in gray knickerbockers, and a blue flannel shirt, with white anchors worked in the corners of the sailor-shaped collar. As for the king, but a short time before he had been only a rollicking little fellow astride of a cherry tree bough, and a blue-eyed little Nan had stood holding out her apron to catch the cherries he threw down, and gazing up at him with a face full of wonder at his daring. But the old and brittle bough had suddenly given way under his weight, and Reginald Fairfax tumbled in a sad little heap to the ground.

Quick as a flash Nan sat down by his side, with her feet straight out before her, and drew the brown head into her lap, while the tears fell fast on the face that seemed so still and lifeless. Her brother Harry ran for the young doctor up at the hotel, as fast as his stout little legs could carry him.

All this had happened only last week, and now Reginald lay on a hospital cot in his own little room in the cottage, and Harry and Nan were waiting on the porch till the doctor should come out and they could be admitted.

They were both very quiet, for they had not seen Regie since the accident, and were awed at the thought of being soon ushered into his presence. Harry kept making round holes in the gravel path with the heel of his boot; Nan sat staring in abstracted fashion at a little wreath of oak leaves which she was balancing on one extended hand.

Presently the doctor came out. "You can go up now," he said, "Regie expects you." Then he caught up his tennis racquet, which he had left on the porch, and hurried away, for the doctor was taking his vacation. If he had not been quite a young doctor, perhaps he would rather have forgotten for those two short weeks that there was such a thing as a patient in the world. But as matters stood he did not seem to mind in the least, that now and then he must stop whatever he was doing, and run over to see "how the little Fairfax boy was coming on," and, young as he was, he had set Regie's leg as neatly and dexterously as any older and more experienced surgeon could have set it.

The children crept quietly up the stairway which landed them at Reginald's door.

Nan paused midway in the room and looked toward Regie with a puzzled frown, for the little fellow stretched out on the cot did not seem exactly like the Regie she had known, tumbling around out of doors.

Harry scarcely stirred a foot beyond the door-sill, and screwed his funny round mouth into a funnier pucker, a queer little habit to which he always resorted in moments of embarrassment.

"I'm very sorry for you, Regie," said Nan, drawing a trifle nearer.

The old brittle bough suddenly gave way under his weight, and Reginald tumbled in a sad little heap to the ground.

"It is too bad," replied Regie. "It couldn't be helped though;" a remark which he had volunteered several times, as if anxious that no one should think that carelessness had aught to do with the accident.

"We've thought of a splendid game," said Harry, feeling that he ought to say something.

"I guess the only game I'll play for a good while will be

still pond, no moving," said Regie, with a poor little ghost of a smile.

"Oh! no, indeed," cried Nan, eagerly, "you're to be the principal one in this game. You're to be a little king, and we are to be your body-guard."

"What's a body-guard?" asked Regie, in a tone as though he doubted the merits of everything with which he could not claim previous acquaintance.

"Oh! it's a——, but we are not going to tell many people,"

answered Harry, glancing significantly toward a room opening out of Regie's, where some one, a stranger to him, sat knitting.

"She's only my nurse," Regie explained; "you mustn't mind her, for she'll have to be round a great deal, and you don't catch me having a body-guard unless I know just what it is."

"It won't hurt you," laughed Nan, with her hands behind her back, and still standing in the centre of the room. Harry had made so bold as to take a seat on the edge of a high-backed rocker, so very much on the edge, in fact, that it threatened to land him on the floor any moment.

"Why don't you sit down, Nan?" Reginald asked at last.

"I can't sit down, Regie, because of the crown," and Nan looked beseechingly toward Harry, as if acting under orders.

"Yes, you may show it now," was Harry's patronising answer; whereupon Nan exultingly held up the little oak wreath before Regie's wondering gaze.

"Oh! is that the crown?" and Regie betrayed a shade of disappointment in his tone, having a conviction that such articles ought to be made of gold, or at least of silver.

"Oh! Regie, don't you like it? It took me a whole day to make it," Nan exclaimed, with a perceptible quiver in her voice.

"Oh yes, it's very nice, very nice indeed! only—well! it'll wither, you know."

"I can make another then," she said, complacently, as though that objection were easily met. "May I put it on your head?"

"Certainly;" and Regie bent his head forward from the pillow.

Nan stood in great awe of the apparatus of weights attached to the cot to keep Regie's limb from shortening while the broken bone was knitting.

"Are you sure it won't do your leg any harm?" she asked, nervously, holding the crown, poised in both hands, above his head, for she could only boast eight years, and was rather a timid little body. Regie laughed outright at this, and Harry shouted, "Of course not, goosie!" with true brotherly disgust.

Thus encouraged she dropped the crown on to Regie's head.

"You look lovely in it," she said, bringing the hand-glass from the bureau; "you can lean your head back, it won't hurt the crown."

"It hurts me though," said Regie, settling back against the pillow, and holding the little mirror at arm's length that he might see the general effect; "it pricks."

"I do not think a king ought to mind such a thing as a prick," Nan remarked, seriously, for she possessed a lively imagination, and, for the time being, Regie was a real little king.

"Perhaps not," said Regie, recalling something about "Uneasy lies the head that wears a crown" (which proverb had once been set for a copy in his writing book at school), and thinking how very true it was. "But you have not told me anything about the body-guard," he added.

"As I understand it," said Harry, who liked to use a big word when he could, "the body-guard sort of takes care of the king, and does whatever he tells 'em to do."

"Then you and Nan are to do *whatever* I tell you," with an accent on the "whatever."

"Yes," said Nan, with hearty seriousness. Harry merely nodded his head, as if not quite willing to commit himself by an audible "yes." He looked as though he foresaw some unpleasant possibilities in Regie's "whatever."

"If you think of anything you'd like to have," Nan farther explained, "why, Harry or I will run and get it—and things like that you know."

"My! but that'll be fun for me," said Regie.

"Of course it will," Nan replied; "that's why we thought of it, because there's a great many kinds of fun you'll have to do without while you must lie so still. Will it be for very long, Regie?" she asked, wistfully.

"Pretty long, I guess," answered Regie, with an honest little sigh.

"It was Nan that made it up," said Harry, whose thoughts had a trick of following their own bent independent of other people's; "I don't know as I'm going to like it."

"Like what?" queried Regie, with a puzzled frown.

"Why, the being ordered about."

"Oh, I'll be easy on the body-guard," laughed Regie.

"I'm ashamed of you, Harry Murray, to talk like that right before poor Regie!" and Nan's face showed how real was her mortification.

"I don't believe kings wear their crowns to bed!" exclaimed Regie, having borne the pricking of the stiff little leaves as long as he could. "This king won't, at any rate. Hang it on that nail, Nan, where I can reach it, and put it on whenever you seem to forget that I am the king, and you must mind me," with a sly look toward Harry. Harry's threatened downfall became a reality just at that moment, and the unbalanced rocking-chair landed him suddenly on the floor.

"I think we had better go now," he said, picking himself up, with a furtive look in the direction of the nurse, knowing that such a mishap was rather inexcusable in a sick room.

"I should think we had," observed Nan, with a good measure of reproach in tone and accent; and after a good-bye to Regie, and a friendly word or two from the nurse who had come in with Regie's luncheon, the children took their departure.

Down the path, across the boulevard and over to the beach they trudged, side by side, but without saying a word to each other. Nan was preserving a dignified silence, which means that she wished Harry to understand by her manner that she did not at all approve of his behaviour during their visit. But Harry was so completely absorbed in his own thoughts as to be quite unmindful of the implied rebuke. When they reached the beach he lingered to watch the fishermen bring their boat in over the surf, leaving Nan to walk the rest of the way home alone.

Regie felt tired after his talk with the children, and having eaten the luncheon, soon dropped off into a sound little nap, to dream of kings and queens and all sorts of royal things, suggested, no doubt, by the oak-leaf crown on which his brown eyes were resting the last moment before the long lashes closed over them. In these brown eyes and long lashes lay the charm of Regie's face, and he had reason to be very grateful to them. Perhaps you wonder how this could be? Well, the very next chapter will tell you.

II.

The King holds an interview with Sister Julia

THE second evening after Reginald's accident, Mr. Fairfax sat down by his cot, and taking up his little brown hand, said cheerily, "Well, Master Regie, we shall need to have a nurse for you."

"I should think I was rather too old for that, sick or well," replied Regie, biting his lip, lest unruly tears should betray that he was not so very old after all.

"Why, Reginald," laughed Mr. Fairfax, "grown-up people have nurses when they break their legs, and are glad enough to get them. Your mamma Fairfax will never be able to do all that must be done for you, and Dr. Delano knows of a splendid nurse. He is sure you will like her, and he would be glad to have her come here to the seashore for a while. He says it will do her good as well as you."

So it happened that Sister Julia arrived the very next day, and Regie grew fond of her in almost less time than it takes to tell it. He thought she had the sweetest face he had ever seen, and a good many other people thought so too. She always wore a pretty cap, a little square shawl, and a long full apron, all made of the same soft, white material.

"Of course," thought Regie, "it's all right for a nurse to wear an apron, and I know some children have French nurses with caps; but Sister Julia is not French, and besides, what's the use of the little shawl?" and as was usual when he did not thoroughly understand anything, he soon made inquiries on the subject.

Sister Julia was sitting at the east window of Regie's room, watching two schooners far out at sea, whose sails, aglow with the red light of the sunset, made them look like fairy boats of conkshell. "Oh, Regie!" she said, at last, earnestly, "I never saw the ocean as beautiful as it is to-night. I wish you were able to have me lift you up, so that you could have a look at it."

"I would rather look at you any day," Regie said, honestly, "because you do look lovely in those white fixings, but I do not see very much sense in 'em."

"I'm afraid there isn't very much sense in them, Regie; only that we all wear them."

"All your family?"

"Yes, all my family. And how many do you suppose there are of us?" Regie looked mystified. "There are seventy-five."

Regie looked incredulous, but he had a foolish notion of never liking to appear astonished at anything, so he said quite casually, as though he were asking the most commonplace question, "And are you the oldest of seventy-five?"

"Do you think I look old enough for that?"

"No, not exactly, but your hair is pretty gray, and no one that's young has gray hair, you know."

"You are not far from right, Regie, but gray hair or no, I am not the oldest of my seventy-five sisters. Have you never heard of a Sisterhood,—that is, of a society of women who bind themselves together for some sort of work?"

"Oh yes, often," said Regie, not meaning to be untruthful, but because always averse to pleading ignorance on any subject. At any rate, if he had heard of a sisterhood his ideas were somewhat vague regarding it.

"Well, I belong to such a society, and all who join it pledge themselves to follow its rules, to take the title of Sister, and to wear these white fixings as you call them, and the work of our society is to care for the sick."

"Have you got to do it all your life?" he asked, shaking his brown head from side to side by way of sympathy.

"No, we are not obliged to do it always. We can resign at any time, but most of us love the work so much, that it would be a great trial to give it up."

Regie did not speak for several seconds, then he said, timidly, "Would you not like to be married, Sister Julia?"

"Well, Regie, that depends," she answered, with an amused smile.

"I should think some one would have wanted you. Did nobody ever?"

"These are pretty plain questions, Regie," said Sister Julia, as indeed they were; and then Regie suddenly remembered that Mamma Fairfax had told him, and but a little while ago, too, that he must get the better of this questioning trick of his.

"I did not think you would mind," he said, and his voice trembled a little.

"Oh no, dear! Of course I don't mind; only you see it might be rather embarrassing to have to own up that nobody ever had wanted me."

"But I know somebody did, because——" Regie paused a second, for he was not sure he ought to tell this; but his desire got the better of his judgment, as often happens with older people, "because I overheard Dr. Delano tell Papa Fairfax that somebody did want you, but that you sent him away 'cause you thought you'd better care for sick children."

"It does not matter much, Regie, whether all that is true or not; but I think we have talked quite long enough about me. Let us talk about you a little while."

"Oh, there's nothing particular about me, 'cept that I'm adopted. I suppose you know that, everybody does," with a little sigh, as though he wished everybody didn't.

"Yes, I know; but I do not believe Mr. and Mrs. Fairfax could love you more if you were their own little boy."

"I am their own little boy, too. I mean, I mean——" and without a word of warning Regie burst into tears.

An unusually sweet look of sympathy came into Sister Julia's face just then, as she moved her rocking-chair close to the cot, and began stroking Regie's hair, for he was crying too hard for her to attempt to reason with him. Her heart went straight out to this high-strung, sensitive boy, and she was sorry enough in any way to have grieved him. By-and-by, when the tears were somewhat under control, he said, with a little convulsive sob between every two or three words—

"I know you did not mean to say anything, but I could not help crying. Some folks, you know, thinks there isn't any good in adopted children. It's an awful pity fellows can't choose their own fathers and mothers; I'd have chosen Papa and Mamma Fairfax every time, and then I could have called them just papa and mamma the way other children do. I do wish they'd never told me about it," and the tears threatened to overflow again.

"Ah, Regie," said Sister Julia, quietly, "you know that they have taught you to call them Papa and Mamma Fairfax only because they feel they have no right to the very same names as you would have used for your own father and mother, if they had lived."

"Yes, I know," he answered, sadly.

"Regie, I would like to tell you a story. Do you feel like listening?"

A sort of little after-sob helped to give Regie's head a forward shake which meant, yes, he would like to listen.

"Well, about thirty years ago, a little girl was left quite alone in the world. Her father, a young physician, and her mother, were both taken away in one week by a terrible fever, which had broken out in the village in which they lived. At first there seemed to be no one to care for the little girl, but after a while a lady, whose baby had died with the fever, offered to take her; and oh, how kind she was to her for years and years, and the little girl never dreamed that she was not her very own mother. Well, it happened one day at school, when the little girl was twelve years old, that an unkind boy called to her: 'Say, Julia, you're only adopted, aren't you?' Only adopted, what could he mean? The words kept ringing in Julia's heart, and at recess she slipped away and ran home as fast as she could."

"'It is not true that I am only adopted, is it, mamma?' she said, as she rushed into the house."

"'Yes, yes, it is true,' said her mother, sadly; 'but who has told you about it, Julia?' The little girl did not answer; she cried and cried and could not be comforted. 'Why did you not tell me yourself, mamma?' she sobbed over and over again."

Sister Julia paused a moment to run the window shade up to the top, so that Regie could see the evening star growing bright in the deepening twilight.

"I should not wonder," said Regie, "if we were talking about you again, Sister Julia."

"I should not wonder if we were, so you see I know just how to feel for you; only I think it is better always to have known the facts as you have done, than to have it come suddenly upon one, and perhaps as roughly as it did upon me."

Regie laid his hand over in Sister Julia's lap, "I'm awfully glad you were adopted," he said, stroking her hand affectionately.

"Why, dear child?"

"Oh, because—well—I shall never be ashamed of it now, I guess. I used to think it was kind of disgraceful, and that it made a difference in a fellow's looks somehow; but I'm sure it doesn't in yours."

"Oh, Regie! what a foolish notion," and Sister Julia laughed merrily.

"I did though," said Regie, "really."

"Do you know, Regie, I think you ought to be one of the happiest children in the world, and you yourself know why."

"Well, I suppose," said Regie, thoughtfully, "that I ought to remember how different it would have been if they had not taken me, and that ought to make me very happy; and, Sister Julia, I am happy, almost always. Anyhow, I guess I'll never be unhappy again about being adopted. I do love Papa and Mamma Fairfax dearly; nobody knows how much," and Regie's face glowed and his eyes kindled with loyal affection. Speaking of eyes, a promise at the end of the last chapter must not be forgotten. Regie owed a particular debt to these brown eyes and long lashes of his, because when he was but a little baby, and while his own mother was living, they had won his way right into Mrs. Fairfax's heart, and so, when he was left an orphan, what more natural than that they should win his way right into her arms as well.

III.

The Fairfaxes call on the Murrays

REGIE'S accident had happened late in June, and the weeks had worn slowly away with their dull monotony varied by many a visit from loyal Nan and Harry. Now, it was the middle of August, and Regie was about again, only with an addition to the body-guard in the shape of two sturdy little crutches. It happened one evening about this time, when Regie had been stowed away for the night, that Mr. Fairfax was walking up and down in front of his cottage in a "brown study," which means, you know, that he was thinking too hard about something in particular, to pay any attention to things in general. It seemed a pity he should not discover in what a glory of gold and crimson the sun was setting, and how beautiful its reflection over on Pleasure Bay. Then a party of the neighbours' boys were engaged in some dexterous and pretty bicycle-riding a little way up the road, and he was missing that also.

Hereward, a greyhound, only he was fawn-coloured instead of gray, and Ned, a Gordon setter, would now and then come bounding up to their master, expecting to be petted, and look strangely surprised when he took no notice of them. They would plant their forefeet in the ground, with their heads on one side, in a questioning, beseeching manner, and stand gazing up for a moment into his face, but only for a moment; there were too many circles to be described, and too many matters to be looked into, to waste much time upon such an indifferent master. Presently the click and bang of a swinging screen door roused Mr. Fairfax from his reverie, and he hurried to join his wife, who had just come out from the house.

She was a lovely little woman, this Mrs. Fairfax, with a face not unlike Sister Julia's, and whether joy or pathos found most expression in her clear gray eyes no one could discover.

She had no sooner stepped on to the piazza, than Hereward and Ned were fairly leaping upon her. There was a little shawl on her arm, and a lace scarf on her head, which they well knew meant a walk to the beach, and, from their point of view, nothing quite compared with that.

"I do not need to ask what you have been thinking about, Curtis," Mrs. Fairfax said to her husband, when they had gone but a little way; "you are wondering and wondering, and so am I, whatever we shall do with Regie."

"It has been a puzzling question, Alice," said Mr. Fairfax; "but I believe I am prepared to answer it. I think the best thing we can do will be to leave him here at the beach."

"Why, Curtis dear, that is simply impossible," Mrs. Fairfax replied, in a decided little way of her own; "there will not be a cottage open here two months from now."

"I know of one cottage, at any rate," said her husband, "that is open all the year round, and where Reginald and Sister Julia would be likely to have a very happy time of it while we are away."

"Of course, you mean Captain Murray's."

"Of course I do. Don't you agree with me about its being a good place, and had we not better walk right up there now and see if they will consider it?" They had come to the railroad crossing, and the shrill whistle of a locomotive brought them to a standstill. Seldom an express train went spinning through Moorlow that Hereward did not run a race with it, and the engineers on the road were always on the lookout for him. Hereward was a very knowing dog; he would lie dozing in the sun, and let the local trains steam up to the little station and off again, without so much as cocking up an ear, but would detect the approach of the "express" way down the track. To-night proved no exception to the rule. Mr. and Mrs. Fairfax watched him proudly, as in a flash he gathered himself together and started for the race. For fully a quarter of a mile he held his own, and, if he had possessed as inexhaustible a supply of breath as the iron-chested engine, his long limbs might sometimes have won him the victory.

As for Ned, this sort of thing was not at all to his taste, and he stood looking stolidly on, as much as to say, "Great waste of time and energy."

Between you and me, had his body been as long, and his legs as slender as Hereward's, he would probably have joined in the wild scamper. There are people here and there in the world not at all unlike Ned; they sit and frown upon certain innocent pleasures simply because they are not fitted by nature to enjoy them.

Breathless and satisfied, Hereward was soon back again, trotting and sniffing along as though nothing had happened.

"I do not believe we had better go to Captain Murray's to-night," said Mrs. Fairfax, taking up the conversation where the train and Hereward's performances had interrupted it; "I would like time to think it over."

"Oh, I've thought it over enough for both of us, Alice. Besides, you see, we must decide upon some plan pretty quickly; it is only ten days now before we sail."

So Mr. and Mrs. Fairfax kept on down the beach, climbed the short flight of wooden steps that scaled the bulk-head in front of Captain Murray's cottage, and knocked at the door. Mrs. Murray opened it.

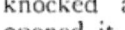

"Why, how do you do?" she said, with evident surprise and pleasure, as she ushered them into the sitting-room. Hereward and Ned poked their noses in at the door, and acted as though they intended to crowd their bodies in too. One look from Mr. Fairfax seemed to change their minds, and with grave faces and limp tails they lay down on the porch instead.

"Here, Harry, bring a chair for Mrs. Fairfax," said Mrs. Murray, "and Nan, darling, go call your father."

This little sitting-room was the very cosiest, perhaps, that one would find from end to end of the whole Jersey shore. Cheery and cool-looking in this summer weather, with the linen floor covering and the vines at the windows, and so warm and cheery in the fall and winter, with pine logs blazing on the old brass and irons.

"Father's coming," announced Nan, returning to the room. "And how's Regie?" asked both the children in one breath.

"Oh, he's getting along finely," answered Mr. Fairfax.

"I'm *right glad* to hear *that*," said Mrs. Murray, who always conversed with strong accents on certain words. "And it's a good piece of news to carry to bed and dream over," she added, turning to the children, and looking toward the energetic little clock on the mantel-shelf. "Come, it's high time; a good-night to Mr. and Mrs. Fairfax, and a kiss for your mother." The children mechanically obeyed, and with reluctant, backward glances trudged up the winding stairway leading directly from the sitting-room.

"Well, well," exclaimed Captain Murray, a wiry, weather-beaten man, as he entered the room, "a call from the Fairfaxes; what's up, I wonder?"

"Seems to me, you're pretty free, father," said Mrs. Murray, half apologetically.

"Well, something is up," replied Mr. Fairfax, "one may as well be honest. We have a proposition to make, and we are very much afraid you won't accept it, and then we shall be all at sea again."

"Oh, I see," laughed Captain Murray, "you want an old sailor to bring you into port, or something like that, eh? Well, if there's anything we can do for you——"

"There is something," said Mr. Fairfax, eagerly, "and a pretty big something too. We want to know if you will take Reginald and Sister Julia into your own snug little harbour for three or four months. You know, when we adopted Regie, Mrs. Fairfax promised that he should never stand between us——"

"He means," interrupted Mrs. Fairfax, thinking she could better explain matters, "that if ever the question came up of remaining with Curtis or Reginald, the decision should always be in favour of my husband."

"That is the way of it," said Mr. Fairfax, "and at last the question has come up. I am obliged to go to Europe for three or four months, and I have no notion of putting that great ocean yonder between my wife and me. Of course, Reginald is not in a condition to travel, and we have been greatly at a loss to know what to do with him. This would be such a fine place for him, if you only would be good enough to let us board him with you."

"I don't know much, after all, about the domestic harbour," said Captain Murray, with elevated eyebrows. "You must ask the first-mate. What do you say, Mollie Murray?"

"Do you think we could really make him comfortable, father?" asked Mrs. Murray, smoothing out her white apron; "we live very plain, and the boy has been accustomed to ——"

"Comfortable! Oh, Mrs. Murray," interrupted Mrs. Fairfax, "why this seems to me altogether the most *comfortable* little home that I know of, and Reginald will be so happy here with the children. As for Sister Julia, I am sure she will be a help rather than a trouble, and you will fairly love her before she has been in the house twenty-four hours."

After this the conversation fell into a quiet chat between the "women-folk," and a more business-like one between Mr. Fairfax and Captain Murray, and when, in its thumping, ringing way, the little clock struck nine, everything had been arranged to the satisfaction of everybody.

"I cannot tell you what a load is off my mind," said Mrs. Fairfax, pressing Mrs. Murray's hand in both of hers, as she stood ready to go. "I only hope it has not rolled off on to yours."

"Never you fear, dearie," Mrs. Murray answered, in her cheerful, whole-souled way.

"How about Hereward and Ned?" exclaimed Mr. Fairfax, almost stumbling across both as they lay on the porch. "And how about Reginald's pony? Can you care for them too, Captain Murray?"

"Yes, yes, send 'em along. We'll do our best by all hands."

"Oh, Mrs. Murray," said Mrs. Fairfax, turning back for a moment, "please don't tell the children about the plan. Regie would so much enjoy telling them himself."

"Oh, to be sure," she answered; "I'll not say a word. Happy secrets are hard things for me to keep; but I'll keep this, I promise you."

THE FAIRFAXES CALL ON THE MURRAYS.

The two dogs who had come over in such rollicking fashion, trotted back again quietly enough, but Mr. and Mrs. Fairfax felt half inclined to dance all the way home, so delighted were they over the success of this splendid plan for Regie.

IV.

A Surprise for the Body Guard

TRULY no one ever looked into a face more beaming than Regie's when Mrs. Fairfax told him of their plan to leave him in Sister Julia's care, and that they were both to board at the Murrays.

"I've been wondering what you would do," said Regie. "I knew you could not take along a boy on crutches; and, Mamma Fairfax," he added, ruefully, "I thought I was in the way for once at any rate."

Then Mrs. Fairfax drew the little fellow into her lap, and said, very tenderly and earnestly, "Remember this, Regie Fairfax: you have never been in the way yet, and you never will be so long as you stay the dear good boy you are to-day." A grateful, happy look came into Regie's face, and he nestled his head close down on Mamma Fairfax's shoulder, quite forgetting that nine-year-old boys are supposed not to care in the least for that sort of thing.

Well, the day for the move to the Murrays dawned at last, though at times it had seemed to Regie as if it never would come.

In the thought that he was going to live in the same house with Nan and Harry, the little reprobate almost forgot he was to say good-bye to Papa and Mamma Fairfax for three whole months at least. But Mr. and Mrs. Fairfax were quite willing he should forget it, and were only too delighted to see the little fellow anticipating so much happiness. It would have been sad enough to have sailed away over that great ocean, leaving a broken-hearted as well as a broken-legged little Reginald behind them.

Still dependent upon his crutches, Regie of course could not help very much with the packing, but as he sat on the piazza, in the warm September sunshine, Sister Julia gave him a lapful of his own neckties to sort over and fold into a box. They were to move that very afternoon. It was half-past eleven now, and at twelve Harry and Nan were coming, as they thought, to say "Good-bye."

Puzzled little Nan and Harry! They had not heard a word of Reginald's coming to stay with them. Had they known it, they would not have been trudging sorrowfully along the beach as they were that very moment. Naturally they wondered at the strange preparations going forward at home. Fresh dimity curtains had been tacked up in the room over the kitchen, and there was a new bowl and pitcher on the wash-stand, and some red-bordered towels that were very beautiful in Nan's eyes. But when the children asked their mother the reason for all this, she had told them that times were a little hard, as indeed they were, and that they were going to take a couple to board.

"I don't like the idea of a couple to board at all," Harry had confided to Nan when they were gathering up the chips one morning in the woodshed.

"Neither do I," sighed Nan, "but if times are hard of course we ought to make the best of it." That Sister Julia and Reginald were the couple never entered their foolish little heads for a second.

Regie sat sorting the neckties, putting the worn ones, and the ones he did not like, at the bottom of the box, you may be sure. Now and then he would stop to watch the four Brooks' boys, who were playing tennis in front of their cottage, and then it seemed as though he could not stand keeping still another moment; but he knew he must, and that word *must* is a very tyrannical and exacting little master. Presently the waggon from the store at Atlanticville, where they sold everything, from kerosene oil to shoe-strings, drove up and stopped; and a little errand

boy, no larger than Regie, jumped down and pulled a basket out from the back. The basket was filled with groceries, and was so very heavy that the boy had to slip the handle way up to his elbow, so that he could rest part of its weight on his hip, as he carried it into the Brooks's kitchen.

When he came out again he stopped to watch the little tennis players with such a wistful look on his thin face, while the old horse, as overworked as his child-driver, improved the opportunity for a hurried browsing on the Fairfax terrace.

"What a difference!" thought Regie, noting the contrast between the boys in knickerbockers and polo caps and this shabby little stranger. "I wonder why some boys have to wear themselves out trudging round with dinners for other boys who do nothing but have a good time the whole summer long!"

In another moment the little fellow jumped into his waggon, and, as if to make up for lost time, jerked the old horse into a bobbing sort of gait, which was something better than a walk and yet could not honestly be called a trot Then Reginald sat dreaming and looking out to sea. Perhaps he was thinking of a time when there might be a better order of things, not exactly of a better world,—that blue ocean and cloud-flecked sky were about as beautiful as anything could be—but of a time when the sins and misfortunes of the fathers should no longer be visited upon the children, and when everyone should have an equal chance. At any rate his thoughts were far away from anything about him, and Harry and Nan came nearer and nearer, without his ever seeing them, and he only knew they were there when Nan rushed up in front of him and said "Boo!" as if to frighten him out of his reverie.

"Why, I did not see you at all!" exclaimed Regie.

"Of course you didn't; you were looking right over our heads," said Harry, seating himself on the edge of the piazza, and straightway beginning to whittle on a block, which was fast being converted into a boat hull. "You seem to be able to see farther than anyone I know of," he added. "You looked then as though you were staring right round the world and up the other side." Reginald blushed a little. Somehow or other, in the presence of matter-of-fact Harry, he always felt ashamed of this dreaming habit of his.

"We're awful sorry you're going," said Nan. "It's so dull for bodyguards when there's no king to care for."

"I'm glad you're sorry," said Regie, biting his lip to keep from smiling. He did not want to have the pleasure of telling them over quite yet. Then there was a lull in the conversation. It was going to be very lonely without Regie, and the bodyguard, particularly Nan, had little heart for conversation.

"How's your base-ball club getting on, Harry?" asked Reginald, feeling he must either keep matters going or tell right away. "It was great fun your beating those fellows up at the Branch."

"It was quite a beat," Harry replied, complacently, "but I guess our beating days are over."

"Why?" asked Regie, astonished.

"Oh, our catcher, the best in the 'nine,' you know, is disabled."

"That's too bad, but I suppose he'll get over it," said Regie, cheerily.

"Well, I rather guess not," Harry drily remarked; "he's dead," and he held the little boat-hull at arm's length to get a better view of its shape. If Nan had been paying attention she would have taken Harry to task for speaking in such apparently heartless fashion of poor little Joe Moore's death. But instead of listening, she was wondering when would be the best time to give Regie a little rubber pencil-case her right hand was affectionately clasping, as it lay in the bottom of her pocket. There was another long pause, and Reginald could keep his secret no longer.

"Children," he said, importantly, "where do you suppose I am going to when I leave here?"

"To New York, of course," replied Nan, with a little sigh.

"No, sir'ree; to Captain Epher Murray's;" and Regie, glancing from one puzzled face to the other, fairly beamed with delight.

"To our house?" said Nan, incredulously.

"By Jimmini!" exclaimed Harry, tossing his hat so high in the air that it caught on the leader of the roof.

"It isn't so!" said Nan, decidedly, and shaking her head from side to side, showing that she believed that to be one of the things literally too good to be true.

"Yes, it is true," said Sister Julia, who had just come on to the porch with her arms full of boxes; "and I am coming too, and the pony, and Hereward, and Ned."

"And we're going to stay till Christmas," chimed in Regie.

"And what is more," added Sister Julia, "we are coming this very day, and you have arrived just in time to escort the king in person, as a true bodyguard should. His little Royal Highness will ride in his own court carriage," and as she spoke Pet and the village cart jogged up to the door.

Then for a few moments Sister Julia and Nan busied themselves, stowing away in the cart such valuable commodities as two or three tennis racquets, a base-ball bat, a tool chest, a small photographing camera, and other things too numerous to mention. Meanwhile Harry, to use his own expressive English, had "shinned up" one of the piazza posts, and succeeded in regaining his jubilant hat.

Nan's brown little face as she bustled about was wreathed in smiles, but she said nothing. Awhile ago she was too sorry to talk, and now she was too happy.

Finally, Sister Julia helped Reginald into the cart, and Nan, with Regie's crutches in her lap, took her seat on one side and Harry on the other.

"When is your mother going?" questioned Harry.

"To-morrow morning early," Reginald replied.

"Well, don't you want to say good-bye to her?"

"Do you suppose I'd be going off like this, Harry Murray, if I were not going to see her again?" with as much imperiousness as a real king.

"Mr. and Mrs. Fairfax are coming to your house to-night to supper," Sister Julia explained.

"They are, are they?" said Harry, somewhat gruffly. "Well, I think they might have told Nan and me something about it all."

"Oh! I don't," Nan cried, eagerly. "I think s'prises are lovely. I love to be s'prised."

"And I love to s'prise people," said Reginald; "and so Mamma Fairfax planned for me to do it."

"Now I guess you're all ready," Sister Julia remarked, wisely changing the subject, as she tucked the linen lap-robe close about Nan, so that her stiffly-starched little gingham dress should not puff out against the wheel.

"Where are the dogs?" asked Harry, looking forward to their establishment in his home with possibly as much interest as to that of their little master.

Regie gave a loud, shrill whistle. That was one of the few things he could do just as well as before he broke his leg, and so he seemed to take special delight in doing it. Hereward and Ned came bounding from some point back of the house, and Pet, seeming to understand that all was in readiness, started off of his own accord. Hereward and Ned, comprehending at once that they were to be allowed to follow, flew hither and yon in the wildest manner, bringing up at the cart every few minutes as if to report proceedings.

"Regie, why do you always say Papa Fairfax and Mamma Fairfax, instead of just papa and mamma?" Nan asked presently. Evidently she had been turning the matter over in her mind for some seconds.

"Because—because—" Regie hesitated,—"because, don't you know, I'm adopted."

"'Dopted," said the children, in one breath. Reginald nodded his head in the affirmative, and sat thoughtfully watching the sand as it fell from the wheel with each revolution. If he had looked into Nan's face or Harry's he would have seen a world of wonder in it.

Finally Nan said, in a very sympathetic way, as though she felt it must be something very dreadful,—

"I do not know just what being adopted means, but have you always been so?"

"Almost always. You see, Nan, my own father died when I was a little fellow, and then Papa Fairfax, who was my father's best friend, took me for his own little boy; and that being took is being adopted."

In certain earnest moments Regie often forgot all about grammar.

"O—h!" said Nan.

It is astonishing how much that one word may mean when one gives it the right inflection. As Nan used it, it stood for "Yes, I understand now; you need never say another word about it, but isn't it strange? Not your own father and mother! I shall have to do a great deal of thinking about that."

By this time Pet had travelled the half mile between the cottages, but without doubt Hereward and Ned had made two miles of it. Regie half believed they had understood the conversations going on about them, and knew that they were to be permitted to enjoy, for three months longer, the freedom of their life by the sea, instead of being cooped up in the cramped backyard in town. At any rate, they were a pair of very jolly dogs that warm September morning.

V.

Goodnight and Goodbye

IT was quite an event in the Murray family to have such people as the Fairfaxes come to supper, and perhaps it was not strange that great preparations were being made; but you might have thought that Mrs. Murray expected Mrs. Fairfax to go straight through her cottage on a tour of critical inspection. The whole house was put in *apple-pie* order—whatever that may mean— from the cool, clean-smelling cellar, to the little triangular attic, redolent of thyme and sage and other dried things hanging from the rafters. Not that there was ever much disorder in that neat little household; but the fact that the Fairfaxes were coming seemed to lend an extra touch of thoroughness to everything that Mrs. Murray did.

Soon after the children's arrival Sister Julia knocked at the door, and was warmly welcomed. She busied herself right away with unpacking the trunks, which had been sent down that morning, while Regie sat at the pretty curtained window of the room that was to be his, telling Sister Julia where to put his own particular treasures. Already he was fond of that little window, from which he could look straight out to sea.

Nan was busy in the kitchen, cutting out the thinnest of little round cookies from dough that her mother had mixed. Some of them were already in the oven, and sending such a delicious savoury smell up into Regie's room!

Harry was active, making things comfortable for Ned and Hereward in the barn.

It was a very happy afternoon all round, though withal a trifle sad too; for there is always something in the atmosphere more or less depressing on the eve of any decided change, no matter how satisfactorily everything may have been arranged for everybody. At six o'clock Mr. and Mrs. Fairfax came down the beach, and at half-past six supper was on the table. Such an inviting little supper-table, with its snowy cloth, polished plated service, and shining glass lamp in the centre, to say nothing of innumerable good things to eat, including a dish heaped high with a delicious "floating island," such as few besides Mrs. Murray know how to make. The canary, in his cage over the plants, was

HARRY

singing away for dear life, as if he wanted to make the occasion just as merry as possible; and Hereward and Ned, who must have sniffed the buttered toast and broiled mackerel from outside, scratched away at the door trying to gain admission. Then they bounded to the window, and planting their paws upon the sill, peered in with a most beseeching look on their intelligent faces. I wonder what they thought of what they saw?

The family were standing at their places at the table with their heads bowed, and Captain Murray was asking a blessing, a long blessing with a little prayer midway, for the dear friends going on so "distant a journey."

Ah! Ned and Hereward, there lies the difference; true and loving and grateful as you are, you cannot comprehend that there is a Father in heaven willing to hear and answer the prayer of every soul He has created.

"Let the good fellows in to-night," said Captain Murray, when the blessing was over, and he discovered the dogs at the window. Harry unlatched the door only too gladly, and they came leaping in; but acting under orders from their lord and master, soon dropped quietly down in one corner to wait as patiently as possible for their own supper time. Regie sat next to Mamma Fairfax, holding his fork in the wrong hand now and then, that he might give her left hand a squeeze under the table. Regie was happy and contented, and yet there was a real little ache in his heart. She was going a long way from home, that dear Mamma Fairfax of his, and how could he help feeling somewhat sad about it?

Mr. Fairfax was apparently very full of fun that night, and amused the children, telling of certain strange pranks of his own when he was a boy.

Mrs. Murray laughed whenever the others did, but she really did not hear much that was going on, she was so thoroughly preoccupied in seeing if Mrs. Fairfax would not have another biscuit, or if Mr. Fairfax's cup was empty, and in caring that everyone had plenty to eat. When supper was finished, Sister Julia in her quiet, helpful way insisted upon aiding Mrs. Murray to clear the table. Little Nan attended to her regular share of the work, and as a result, soon paraded a wonderfully bright row of tumblers on the lowest shelf of the dresser. When the red cloth had been laid on the table, Captain Murray brought out a great map, and they all gathered about while Mr. Fairfax showed them the plan of their journey.

"You'll get it out often and keep track of us, won't you?" he said to Regie, taking the crutches from his hand and lifting him to his knee.

"Every night," Regie promised, solemnly.

"Not every night, Rex," said Mr. Fairfax. "That will not be necessary, because you see we shall spend a week in London, and another whole week in Berlin, and two weeks perhaps in Paris."

"Shall you?" asked Regie, ruefully.

"Why, to be sure; have you any objections, Rex?"

"Oh, I thought you'd keep going and going until you got back again. I shall not like to think of you as stopping so long anywhere."

"We shall come home just as soon," laughed Mr. Fairfax, giving that little adopted boy of his the most genuine sort of a fatherly hug.

All too soon it was nine o'clock, and time for the children to go to bed.

Mrs. Fairfax went up herself with Regie. Sister Julia had been up before her and lighted the candle, and laid Regie's night-dress out on the bed.

"You will try not to give Mrs. Murray any trouble, won't you, dear?" said Mrs. Fairfax, helping Regie to undress.

"Yes, I will, Mamma Fairfax," Regie answered, with a little quiver in his voice.

"And you will write to me once a week?"

"Yes, mamma," with two little quivers.

"And you will do just as Sister Julia tells you?"

"Yes," and with a great sob Regie hid his face on her shoulder.

"Why, Rex darling, do you really care so much?" said Mrs. Fairfax, with tears in her own eyes. "Well, I am proud that you do, and you will be all the more glad to have us home again. In the meantime, you will be very happy in this dear little home with Harry and Nan."

"Yes, I know I will," said Regie, with a shadow of a smile.

"And your little crutches will be hanging on the wall long before that time, because you will have no further need of them."

"Yes, I know," said Regie, with a face almost wreathed in smiles at the thought, as he scrambled into bed.

Then Mr. Fairfax ran up the little flight, two steps at a time, to bid him good-bye.

There was considerable whispering and hugging between the little fellow inside the bed and the big fellow outside, and then in another moment Papa Fairfax was gone.

And then it was Mamma Fairfax's turn. "I will send Sister Julia right up," she said, for Regie should not be left alone that night. "And now two of your best hugs and five of your best kisses—and now, my own dear little Rex, good-night and good-bye."

VI.

⸻ In the Highland Light. ⸻

T nine o'clock Thursday evening Mr. and Mrs. Fairfax had bade farewell to their friends at Moorlow. At nine o'clock Friday morning the train whirled by on its way to Sandy Hook, and then they waved good-bye from the car windows, as they had promised, to Regie and Harry and Nan, who, seated on a pile of railroad ties, had been watching and waiting for the train a long half hour. At nine o'clock Saturday morning Mr. and Mrs. Fairfax went on board the *Alaska*, which some one has called "the greyhound of the sea," and a half hour later the good ship steamed out into the Bay.

"Well, I suppose you've seen the last of 'em," said Captain Murray, joining the little party just as the train had disappeared, and looking closely at Regie to see how he was taking it.

"The last for a while, I suppose, sir," said Regie, in a firm little voice, but nevertheless gazing very wistfully down the track in the direction of the vanishing train. "I would have given a good deal," he added, "to have seen the big ship they are going in."

"You would? Well, why not?" said the captain. "Yes, why not?" looking from one puzzled face to the other in an amused sort of fashion.

"Oh!" said Harry, "do you mean that you'll take us to the Highland Light?"

"Of course I do. Where else, to be sure? We can drive over with Dobbin early to-morrow morning. I'll take the glass along, and we'll have a good look at the *Alaska*, every one of us. What time does she leave the dock, Reginald?" for the honest captain believed in calling people and things by their right names.

"Half-past nine, sir," said Regie, promptly, for he was well posted on all the details of the projected journey.

"Then she'll round the Hook about eleven."

"Is the lighthouse very high?" asked Regie, his face aglow with excitement.

"High enough to see a long way out to sea," answered the captain.

"I was not thinking of that," said Regie, rather ruefully. "I was thinking I could not climb up so very many stairs with these crutches."

"But you can go up mighty easy without them. See! just like this," and Captain Murray caught Regie in his arms as easily as Regie himself would have lifted a kitten. "Bring the crutches, Nan," he added, "there's no use in staying here any longer."

"I believe Papa and Mamma Fairfax would like to know we were looking at them," said Regie, with his arms clasped firmly round the captain's neck. "They could not see us, but they could know we were there."

"To be sure," said the captain, making use of those three monosyllables on every possible occasion; "and we'll stop at the railroad station on our way home now, and telegraph them to be on the lookout for us."

"You're a magnificent captain!" said Regie, never hesitating to express honest admiration.

"I'm glad you think so," replied the captain, tightening his hold of the warm-hearted little fellow, "but unfortunately your saying so does not make it true."

"But, papa, it is true," said Nan, loyally, catching hold of her father's coat, and trudging along by his side. "All the men say so at the Life-saving Station, and I guess they ought to know."

"None of them have ever been to sea with me, Nan."

"They know about you all the same," said Harry, with a significant shake of his head; for he was very proud of his tall father, and of his handsome weather-beaten face.

They had reached the little Gothic railroad station, and Captain Murray sat Regie down on the operator's table while he wrote this telegram on one of the yellow paper blanks:—

"MR. CURTIS FAIRFAX,
"No. —, Wall St., New York.

"*The children will wave you good-bye from the Highland Light at eleven o'clock to-morrow, rain or shine.*
"EPHER MURRAY."

Captain Murray caught Regie in his arms as easily as Regie would have lifted a kitten. Nan caught hold of her father's coat, and trudges along by his side.

In two hours back came this answer:—

"Captain Epher Murray,
"Moorlow, New Jersey.
"*Good for you. Keep a sharp lookout for special signals.*
"C. Fairfax."

"A sharp lookout for special signals!" the words kept ringing in the children's ears.

"What can he mean to do—my darling old Papa Fairfax?" thought Regie, as he dropped off into a sound sleep that night.

At eight o'clock the next morning, Sister Julia and Regie and Nan climbed into the back seat of Captain Murray's waggon, while Harry took the place beside his father in front. Faithful old Dobbin broke straightway into a canter, bound for the "Highland Light," and fortunately for the party there was no "rain," but plenty of "shine" instead. Down the fine boulevard they went, past the fine houses, through Sea Bright, with its queer medley of summer cottages, hotels, and fishermen's huts; then crossing and re-crossing the track again and again, because the drive on that narrow strip of land between the ocean and the Shewsbury river constantly accommodates itself to the curves of the railroad; over the rickety Highland Bridge, stopping to pay toll on the draw; past the bevy of cottages, where a number of actors and actresses have established a little colony of their own; up the steep hill, with the great seams washed in the road by the heavy rains, but wide enough and deep enough to seem more like the work of an earthquake; finally coming to a halt at the gate which opens on the rear of the grand old lighthouse.

"Why, how do you do, captain? Want to show the youngsters through the light?" asked the keeper, appearing in the doorway at the sound of the waggon wheels.

"Want to do more than that," answered Captain Murray, lifting his little party out one by one; "want to see the *Alaska* off for Europe."

"Friends on board?"

"This little chap's father and mother."

"Oh, that's it, is it?" said the keeper. "But what's happened the little fellow?" glancing at Regie's crutches.

"He fell from a cherry tree a few week ago," Sister Julia explained, as they walked towards the house.

"Stealing cherries, eh?" chuckled the man, giving Regie a significant little nudge.

"Indeed, I wasn't," answered Regie, with some indignation.

"Why, Reginald, he is only joking," Sister Julia said, reprovingly.

"Of course I was," said the keeper. "Such a bright little fellow as you look to be ought to know when a man's joking."

"Yes, I know I ought," Regie answered, blushing. "I spoke before I thought; you must excuse me, Mr. Keeper."

"'Mr. Keeper,'" laughed the man, "well! that's a new name for Joe Canfield; but I like it, and you're a mighty honest little fellow. When you're ready to go up, you can leave your crutches below here, and I'll carry you over every one of those blessed stairs myself."

"You'd better let papa do that," said Nan, "he's pretty heavy, and we wouldn't have anything happen to him for the world."

"Do you think I would drop him, little one? Never you fear; I could carry you both as well as not;" whereupon Nan started to travel briskly up the stairs, as if to show him she was quite equal to doing her own climbing.

"Bide a bit, miss," called the keeper. "You won't be able to sight the *Alaska* for a half hour yet. If you want to understand about the light you'd better look about down here first." Then he led the way into a room on the ground floor, where the oil for the lights was stored, the little party following him closely, with the exception of Captain Murray, whom the children were glad to have go "on watch" in the balcony of the light, for fear, by any chance, the *Alaska* should be sighted ahead of time.

"I suppose you have noticed before you came in, ma'am," said Keeper Canfield, addressing Sister Julia, "that this lighthouse has two towers and two lights? The dwellings for the keepers' families are in between 'em, and there we live as cosy and comfortable as can be. If you have time when you come down you must take a peep at our baby. Have you ever seen a lighthouse baby?" he added, turning to Nan.

"Never," said Nan, seriously.

"Well, a lighthouse baby is worth seeing, for somehow or other they look brighter than ordinary babies. It seems as though they were born with a notion that their two eyes must cheer us old codgers on life's great sea, just as the lights in the tower there cheer the sailors."

The children looked wonderingly up at their guide, not quite sure whether he were in earnest or no.

"Now, you see," he continued, "this is the room where we store the oil, and how much do you suppose we burn in a year? Forty-five hundred gallons! We burn mineral oil, that is, oil that comes out from the ground through the oil wells."

The room in which they were standing was flanked with wooden boxes, each containing a full oil-can, and everything was scrupulously neat, for not a speck of dust was to be seen anywhere.

"Now I guess we had better go up," said the keeper, when a good many questions had been asked and answered, "and we'll go easy, so as not to lose our breath;" then, taking Regie's crutches in one hand, he lifted him into his arms.

"And, Nan," said Sister Julia, "you had better take hold of my hand, for fear your little head should grow dizzy on this winding flight."

Of course Harry was half-way up before the rest of the party had even started.

The keeper landed Regie safely right inside the light itself, and indeed it was large enough to hold them all. What a marvellous place it was! It seemed as though they were in a beautiful crystal house, for they were surrounded by tier after tier of glass prisms, so arranged as to project the light from the lantern against a series of brass reflectors at the back, and they, in turn, throw the light twenty-five miles out to sea.

The children were too much awed by the wonderful contrivance to even speak, until Harry slipped out of the light and peered in at them through the glass. It made him look very funny— eyes, nose, mouth, every feature appeared to be drawn out lengthwise by the prisms.

"Why, Harry Murray!" cried Nan, "you're a disgrace to the family. I never saw anything so ugly in all my life!"

"I wish you could come out here and have a look at yourself, then," Harry called back. "Your head is about two inches high, and two feet wide. You could stand in a bandbox, you are so short, but it would take a dozen of 'em to hold you the other way!"

Nan and Harry were so much amused with these ridiculous distortions that Reginald was the only one who really paid attention to the keeper's description of the lantern, but he listened sagely, and plied questions fast enough to atone for the indifference of the others. Harry might be partially excused for his inattention, on the ground that he had been through the light two or three times before. As for Nan, it must be confessed that she was not of an inquiring turn of mind.

"There's one sad thing about this light," said the keeper to Reginald, who sat on a little stool with his crutches laid across his knees. "There's one very sad thing, and that is, that some sailors do not understand what it is for at all. They seem to be fascinated by it, and they steer straight for it, and of course there's no help in the end, but that they all get wrecked on the bar."

"Why, that's very queer," said Reginald. "I should think

a man wasn't fit to be a sailor at all unless he understood about lighthouses and things."

"So it would seem," said the keeper, with a shrug; "but I've thought sometimes that the trouble is with their steering apparatus, and that the poor things are more to be pitied than blamed. The moment they come in sight of the light, their helms seem to get bewitched, and first thing they know their queer-rigged little crafts are headed straight for the light, and on they come, sort of in spite of themselves, and with death staring them right in the face."

"Have there been many wrecks lately?" asked Reginald, his eyes as large as saucers.

"Five last night."

Regie stared at the man with a look that meant plainly, "I don't believe a word of it," and the keeper laughed outright. Sister Julia, sitting at the top of the little flight of stairs just outside the lantern, watched him with an amused smile on her face; and Nan, who was listening now, was interested enough to wish that she had heard it all.

"You think that I am telling you a yarn, don't you, youngster?" said the keeper to Regie, "but 'pon honour it is every word true. If you don't believe it, I'll show you the five little wrecks lying in a row on a bench in the yard, just as I picked 'em up this morning."

"Picked 'em up!" said Regie, scornfully.

"Yes, sir, picked 'em up. The reason you don't understand me is because you spell sailor with an "o," but in this case you must spell it with an "e"—sailers, you see—which is only another name for birds, you know."

It was Regie's turn to laugh now. "You fooled me pretty well," he said; but Nan looked more ready to cry.

"Do you mean," said she, "that five little birds flew against this lantern last night, and killed themselves?"

"Five last night, and six the night before," said the man, as though the truth must be told, no matter how unpleasant.

"Ship ahoy!" shouted Captain Murray from the tower

balcony, where he had been on watch for the last half hour. All knew what that meant, and Sister Julia and Nan and Harry hurried down the little flight that led from the lantern to the balcony, and the keeper quickly caught Regie in his arms again.

"Where is she?" cried Regie, impatiently, as though he could hardly wait for an answer.

"You can see her with the naked eye," replied the captain, "away off there in a direct line from the Hook. I knew her build and rig the moment she came in sight; but she's flying a queer sort of flag," putting his glass to his eye.

"Perhaps it's the special signal Mr. Fairfax telegraphed us to look out for," said sister Julia.

"Please let me have a look," cried Reginald, almost pulling the glass from Captain Murray's hands in his eagerness. It took a moment to adjust it to his eyesight, and then he exclaimed, almost breathless with excitement. "Yes, there's a big red flag with some large yellow thing on it. Oh, I know, it's a flag from one of Papa Fairfax's warehouses, and the yellow thing is a coffee canister; see, Captain Murray, see if it isn't."

Captain Murray took the glass back again. "Yes, you're right, Reginald," he said; "but there's something on the flag beside the canister, something that looks like letters."

"Perhaps it is a message," cried Rex, fairly wild with excitement. "Oh! please let me see if I can make them out." Once again the glass was quickly re-adjusted to Regie's sight, while Nan and Harry pressed their faces close to his, as though being as close as possible to the glass was the next best thing to looking through it. "Yes, they are letters," said Regie more calmly, "big white letters, and the first is a G, I think, and the next an O, but the flag waves so I cannot read the rest."

'Perhaps it's 'Good-bye,'" said Nan.

"Of course it is," cried Regie, "I see the B now, and the E; but there's another word besides. Try, Nan, if you can make it out," and Regie with much self-denial gave up his place at the glass.

Wind and tide seemed always to favour little Nan, for at that

very moment a stiff breeze caught the flag and held it out bravely, so that she read "Good-bye, Regie," as easily as from her spelling book at school.

Oh! how the message thrilled through and through Regie's excited little frame. To think that Papa Fairfax cared so much for him as to take all that trouble; and right then and there a prayer went silently up from Regie's full heart that he might never do anything to grieve him—never.

Quickly the glass was passed from one to another that all might have a look.

"Oh, if we only could signal back somehow!" said Sister Julia, earnestly.

"And what is to hinder, dear?" answered the keeper's wife, who had toiled up to the tower with the baby in her arms.

"Daniel," she added, turning to her husband, "run to the parlour and pull down the curtain from the double window. That's big enough for them to distinguish."

Big enough for them to distinguish! you would have thought so could you have seen the great expanse of turkey red that floated from the tower a few minutes later.

"They see it! they see it!" shouted Harry, whose turn it was now at the glass. "They're dipping their colours."

"So they are!" every one cried, for no glass was needed to discern that.

With happy, wistful eyes Regie watched the great *Alaska* till she was a mere speck on the horizon; then the little party turned their faces homeward, and from that moment Regie looked eagerly forward to the day when they should come sailing back again.

VII.

A Trip to Burchard's.

"SEEMS to me, peaches must be at their best about now, father," Mrs. Murray said to the captain, as they sat at breakfast one morning, about a week after Mr. and Mrs. Fairfax had sailed.

"Shouldn't wonder, Mollie," replied the Captain, and then he said nothing more, for he was busy with his own thoughts.

"Shouldn't wondering doesn't help matters any," said his wife at last, impatiently. "What's to be done about 'em, Epher?"

"About what, Mollie?" asked the captain, for he had really forgotten what she was talking about.

"Why! the peaches, to be sure. You must be having one of your absent-minded turns."

"I was thinking, Mollie," he answered, "about getting some new blankets and tarpaulins for the crew. That is more like minding my own business than being absent-minded, it strikes me."

Captain Murray had had charge of the Moorlow Life-saving Station for eight years, and had just accepted a new appointment.

"I guess you'd say I hadn't been minding mine, if I let the fall go by without doing up any peaches. Nobody sets more store by my preserves than you do, Epher Murray, but you'll have few enough to set store by this year, unless you do something pretty quick about 'em."

"Well! well! I'll send word over to Burchard's orchard; that's all that's needed, isn't it?"

"And who will you send, I'd like to know?"

It seemed to Mrs. Murray as though the captain might offer his own services for such an all-important matter as this preserving.

"Couldn't the children drive over for them?" asked Sister

Julia, who always endeavoured to make things as comfortable as possible for everybody.

"The very thing!" Regie exclaimed.

"Oh! do let us go, father," cried Harry and Nan together.

"Of course you can go," answered Captain Murray, only too willing to give a permission that freed him from any responsibility in the matter.

To be allowed to go by themselves all the way to Burchard's orchard seemed quite an adventure in the eyes of the children, and they were anxious to be off, but certain things must needs be first attended to. Nan had various little indoor duties, which kept her busy for a while every morning, and Harry had regular morning work in the neighbourhood of the wood pile. As for Regie, Sister Julia said, kindly but firmly, that "he could not stir a step till he had written a letter to Papa Fairfax." Harry soon succeeded in finishing his task, and hurried out to the barn, as he thought, to help the man, Joe, to put Pet into the harness. What was his disappointment to find the barn empty. He knew in a moment that Joe must have taken him to be shod, for ponies, as well as little people, seem to need shoeing very often, and he rushed back to the house in a great state of excitement.

Regie was struggling with his letter, with Sister Julia sitting by as an authority in the matter of spelling.

"Say," cried Harry, appearing on the scene, "there isn't a sign of Pet in the barn. I s'pose they've taken him off to be shod, and there's no telling when they'll bring him back." His manner showed so very plainly what he thought, that he hardly needed to have added that "he thought it was very mean indeed."

"I think it is very mean, too!" said Regie; "seems to me I ought to be told when my own pony needs shoeing, and not have him walked off just when I want to use him."

"If that is the case you had better off with my head, then, King Regie," laughed Sister Julia; "for I am the guilty one. The moment it was decided that you should go to the orchard I sent Joe off with Pet, for it would never do to have him cast a shoe on such a long drive."

"Oh, that's all right then," said Regie, apologetically. He had a foolish trick of growing indignant over many things, because he would not wait to find out the true facts of a case. This may be said in his favour, however, that when he found himself in the wrong, which was very often, he was always ready to admit it,—an honest, winning trait which is somewhat rare in this self-confident world of ours.

"Now run along, Harry," said Sister Julia. "This letter of Reginald's must go out by to-morrow's steamer, and if he does not hurry, Pet will be at the door long before he is through with it."

Harry departed as requested, and Reginald spread his arms out on the table, and resumed writing, accompanying every up and down stroke of his pen with an earnest little motion of the lips, as if that were a necessary part of the proceeding. With long pauses over certain words, and constant appeals to Sister Julia, frequently as to the spelling of words of which he was perfectly sure, the letter was at last finished, and this was the result—

"MOORLOW, *Sept. 7th*, '85.

"DEAR PAPA FAIRFAX,—We are all well, and having a first-rate time, and hope you are having a good time too. The pony is just as well and fat as ever, but Captain Murray's cow has a very lame foot. We caught a woodchuck last Saturday, and Captain Murray's man, Joe, skinned him, and we gave the skin to Mrs. Murray for a little rug. We have been making darts with horseshoe nails and corks and feathers. Did you know how to do that when you were a little boy? We have had to put the old drake in another place. He kept picking up the little ducks and shaking them. We are going to a peach orchard this morning (if Pet ever comes home from being shod). So good-bye, from
"Your loving
"REGIE.

"P. S. It is very nice here. Captain Murray asked me to send his love to you. Sister Julia is very kind. I love her next to you and Mamma Fairfax.—R. F."

The careful directing of the envelope was the work of an additional five minutes, and Sister Julia stood ready to hand Reginald his hat and crutches the moment it should be completed; for Harry and Nan and Pet were waiting at the door, and all equally impatient.

"Now, children," said Sister Julia, as they were getting stowed away in the cart, "it is eleven o'clock, and it will take you about an hour and a half to drive over, and you must allow the same time for driving home. I shall be worried if you are not here by five. I shall depend upon you, Regie, to keep watch of the time. Let us see if our watches agree." They were found to agree to the minute, and the little party set off. Pet was the most energetic pony; going or coming was all the same to him. He always trotted over the ground as fast as his little legs could carry him, seldom falling into a walk of his own accord. So it was not strange that, with Pet's steady pattering and the children's steady chattering, they found themselves at the peach orchard in what seemed to them a very short space of time, though, in point of fact, they had been on the road almost as long as Sister Julia had predicted.

Regie was able to drive right into the orchard, for the bars of the rail fence had been let down, and they soon came to a rough platform covered with peach baskets, some full and some empty, over which a coloured boy, with hands plunged into his trousers pockets, was loyally keeping guard.

"Any peaches for sale?" asked Harry, scrambling out.

"Lots of 'em," grinned the boy.

"Where's Mr. Burchard?" asked Nan.

"South corner," indicating the direction with a bob of his woolly head; "he's got a gang of men down there with him picking."

"Let's go and help 'em," said Harry, "we can eat all we want to and have lots of fun;" but the words were no sooner uttered than he realised that hobbling over that rough orchard was out of the question for Regie, and indeed it was too rough to drive farther in with the cart.

"One of us must stay with Pet," said Regie, casually, as though there was no other reason in the world why he should not go. Harry and Nan scampered off, with some misgivings on Nan's part as to the kindness of deserting her king; but the vision of a seat on a comfortable bough, with luscious peaches within easy reach, was a stronger test than even her loyalty could bear.

"Want to get out?" said the coloured boy to Rex, when the children had gone. "I'll help you," glancing significantly toward the crutches.

"No, thank you," answered Rex, "it is too much bother;" and, foolish, sensitive little fellow that he was, he blushed up to the roots of his hair, as though a broken leg was something to be heartily ashamed of.

"Lame long?" asked the boy, who seemed averse to wasting breath on any unnecessary words.

"Three months," said Rex, "but I'll soon be over it. I wish you'd let down Pet's check," he added, willing to change the subject.

"Boss pony," said the boy, carrying out Regie's request, whereupon Pet sniffed about him, expecting something to eat.

"Seems hungry," said the boy.

"That can't be," said Rex, proudly; "he has all the hay and oats he wants every day."

"Give him a peach?" asked the boy, with elevated eyebrows.

"Yes, if you want to."

Jim, for that was the boy's name, picked out "a booty," as he called it, gave it rather an unnecessary rub on the side of his old trousers, and popped it into Pet's expectant jaws. Pet made a great fuss over it. It could hardly be an easy matter to manage a large peach, and the good-sized pit inside of it, with a curb bit in the mouth

"Do they give peaches to horses?" asked Reginald, beginning to have some misgivings on the subject.

"Some's feared to do it."

"Are they afraid of the pit's sticking in their throats?"

The boy gave a little grunt that meant "Yes, they were." Regie was alarmed. "But you need not fear 'bout this un," added the boy; "he looks knowin' enough to spit the pit out." Jim was right, and in a few minutes the pit fell softly to the ground. Then the boys fell to talking about one thing and another to while away the time, until it suddenly occurred to Jim to put another peach into Pet's mouth.

"I wish you had not done that," said Regie, a little provoked. "I think he came very near choking on the other one."

There was a sound of wheels just then, and a waggon loaded

with peach baskets came in sight, with Nan and Harry seated in front of them. "There's old black Ned," said Jim, pointing towards the horse that was drawing the waggon; "he eats ten peaches of a mornin,' and spits the pit out every time; but, my eyes! I reckon this pony ain't got sense enough, arter all," for just at this point Pet began to cough and strangle most prodigiously.

"Pull it out, can't you?" said Rex, impatiently, whereupon the boy simply stood and stared, plunging his hands deeper down into the depths of his trousers pocket. Regie knew that he could get to Pet in no other way so quickly as to scramble along his back and drop over his head. It was the work of a moment, and the unexpected arrival of somebody on his neck caused Pet to jerk his head so violently as to send the unlucky stone flying out of his throat, and to land Regie in a topsy-turvy state in front of him. Regie hardly touched the ground before Harry was at his side, trying to help him up. Pet did not know what to make of all this, and stood looking down at his young master with his ears pricked up and his head on one side; but no doubt he was grateful to the transaction that had enabled him to part company with that deplorable stone.

"Your leg's not hurt, is it, Rex?" cried Nan, instantly appearing on the scene.

"I guess not. Get my crutches, please," and Nan hurried to pull them out from under the seat of the cart.

"Why, what's all this?" asked the man, who had been leading the horse with the load of peaches.

"Oh, that old coloured boy of yours gave a peach to my pony, and then, when he choked on the pit, was too much of a coward to try and get it out;" and Rex turned to wither poor Jim with one of his most kingly glances, but Jim had vanished.

"I should think he would take himself off," said Harry, indignantly. "If he'd stayed round here I would have given him a piece of my mind," and Harry made certain significant gestures with the plumpest of fists. "Think of his letting a lame fellow like Rex come tumbling out of the cart, rather than lift his hand to help a choking pony," and an angry red flush shot over Harry's sun-burned face.

Just at this moment Nan discovered a black curly-headed little pate directly under a hole in the platform, but with Harry at this angry pitch she did not dare to make known her discovery. Presently, when Harry and Rex were busy getting into the cart, and the man's back was turned, what did the little witch do but catch up an old tin pail near at hand, dip it half full of powdered dust from the road, and pour it down through that one small hole in the platform. There was a spluttering sound as of suppressed choking. Nan was the only one that noticed it, but her little face was sufficiently wreathed in smiles to prove that "revenge is sweet" to the "gentler sex," though the revenger be still in pinafores.

VIII.

On the way home.

"HEN you will surely send those peaches this afternoon?" said Harry to the man, when all was in readiness to turn their faces homeward.

"Surely; and if you don't hurry up they'll get there before you."

Hurrying was just in Pet's line, and he pricked up his ears as though he fully understood this last remark. Rex gave him the word and away he flew, almost running against the gatepost in his eagerness to be off from that region of coloured boys and peach stones.

"Which way shall we go?" asked Rex, consulting his little silver watch; "we have plenty of time."

"Of course we have," said Nan, "and why shouldn't we stop somewhere when there is an elegant luncheon in the bottom of this cart and we have not taken a minute to eat it?"

"Sure enough," Harry exclaimed, and the children stared at each other with a look of amazement, wondering how it ever could have happened that they should for a moment have forgotten anything so important.

"I tell you what let's do," said Rex; "let's go home by the Rumson Road. I know a lovely great tree, where we can rest Pet while we eat the luncheon."

Harry and Nan fell in with the plan, and Pet, who, with true pony instinct, had started the shortest way home, was obliged to right-about-face. There are not many more charming drives than that of the Rumson Road, bordered as it is on one side by beautiful country houses, whose windows command a near view of the river and a distant one of the sea. Luxuriant hedges and evenly trimmed grass-plots line the drive, and here and there a fine old tree throws a grateful shadow athwart the red soil road. Though each of the little trio had been over it many times before, it seemed to-day to wear a new beauty in their eyes, and when they reached a point where it curves gracefully and two grand old places confront each other, Nan's enthusiasm found vent.

"Isn't it just too beautiful for anything?" she exclaimed.

"Yes, it is lovely," Rex answered,—"just like the country far away from the sea, and yet you can see the ocean as plain as day."

"It is a great pity," said Nan, "that plants and flowers won't grow as they ought to, close down to the shore." She was looking at a great bed of flowers in the midst of one of the lawns, and recalling a little company of spindly geraniums, which she had vainly tried to make flourish in her little garden at home, so depressing is the effect of salt sea-fogs and sandy soil upon all growing things. "And there are no trees to speak of near the sea," she added, with a little sigh, for she dearly loved the green and the shade of the inland country; "nothing but meadows of great coarse grass."

"You forgot the lawns round the places on the boulevard, Nan," said Harry.

"Oh, to be sure, but the grass only grows there because they have men to sprinkle and 'tend to it all the time. Papa says he could s'port half-a-dozen little girls like me for what it costs for one of those lawns a single summer."

"That seems very extravagant," said Regie, who had quite a business way of looking at matters.

"I think I would like to live back here, where things grow as though they loved it, and not because they are made to," Nan remarked, thoughtfully.

"Indeed, I know better, Nannie Murray; you love the sea too much to be contented away from it a week," Harry remarked, with brotherly superiority. "Why, mother took you to Grandma

Murray's when you were only a scrap of a baby, and you cried and fretted so she was ashamed of you, and had to bring you home. The moment you caught sight of the sea you crowed and clapped your little hands, and behaved like another baby altogether. No, sir-ree, you'd be sick of living back here in a week."

"Well, perhaps I would," Nan admitted, for she knew, after all, that no sound was so sweet in her ears as the roar of the breakers on the beach, nor anything that looked quite so beautiful to her as the dear old ocean, whether under a blue sky or a grey one.

By this time they had reached Regie's tree. It stood just at the top of a little descent in the road, and not many yards away from one of the numerous railroad crossings which traverse that part of the country.

Rex was helped out to a comfortable seat under it. Harry took Pet out of the shafts and tied him to a rail fence near by, while Nan, a perfect counterpart of her energetic mother, began transferring the luncheon from the basket to the grass, and spreading it out so that it should look as inviting as possible.

Then there was silence as far as any continued conversation was concerned for the space of fifteen minutes. There was an occasional "These biscuits are delicious," or a "Please pass me the sponge cake," but that was all. A good appetite and plenty to gratify it generally quiets, for the time being, even the most incessant of little chatterboxes.

When the luncheon was all disposed of, save a few crumbs,—which, by the way, made a beautiful meal for a family of ants the next day,—Regie threw himself on his back, and with hands folded under his head, looked up into the boughs, and in dreamy fashion watched the birds flying in and out. Harry whipped the inevitable boat hull out of his pocket and began whittling; and Nan, as any one who knew her could have foretold, soon discovered some sort of wild flowers at a little distance, and wandered off to gather them. They proved to be Black-eyed Susans, as the children call the yellow field daisies; and when she had picked them she discovered a larger growth of the same flower farther on in the midst of one of those luxuriant wild hedges, which often flourish along the line of railroads in the country. Of course she must needs have these too, and she hurried to reach them, as though half afraid that someone would seek to rob her of the prize. Eagerly she broke the stems; with a quiet knack placed each flower just where it would most contribute to the effectiveness of her bouquet, and she was just turning to go back to the boys when she spied something large and dark lying right across the track a hundred yards away.

"Harry! Reginald!" she cried, at the top of her voice, "come here, quick!" at the same time shading her eyes with her hand, to discover, if possible, what the something might be. Harry was on his feet in an instant, for Nan was hidden from sight, and he feared some accident. Regie reached for his crutches and followed after as fast as he could. It seemed to Nan as though Harry never would come. "Look there," she cried, as soon as he was within hearing distance, "What can it be?" pointing down the track as she spoke.

"My jimini, I believe it's a cow!" and, more courageous than Nan, hurried on to investigate. Nan, with a pretty native thoughtfulness, waited till Rex had hobbled up to her, and then they trudged along to join Harry, who had reached the dark object, and stood poking at it with a sharp-pointed stick. Yes, it was certainly a great, dark-red cow, and the little party, gathering around her, stared at her for a few seconds in awe-struck silence.

"Is she dead?" asked Nan, betraying a world of emotion in her voice.

"Looks like it, doesn't it?" said Harry, appealing to Regie. Rex shook his head solemnly in the affirmative.

"Oh, dear, dear!" cried Nan, "she'll be run over when the train comes."

"It won't hurt her if she is," answered Harry, trying to assume a light tone; but his face plainly showed that he thought it a pretty serious matter.

"I wonder what we ought to do?" said Rex.

"I think we had better get right off this track this minute," Nan wisely advised, "for there's no knowing when a train may come round the curve yonder." So they clambered up the bank and sat down to deliberate.

"Do you suppose she will throw the train off the track?" questioned Nan.

"I don't believe so," said Rex, "that's what the cow-catcher is for, you know."

"But the trouble is they don't always catch," remarked Harry, with an emphatic shake of his head.

"Oh, do you suppose a train may be coming?" asked Nan, with a perceptible little shiver.

"How should we know, goosie?" answered Harry, with a nervous sort of shrug.

"But," questioned Rex, in business-like fashion, "what are we going to do about it?"

"Well," said Harry, "I don't see that we can do anything. I haven't an idea where this road can run to. Perhaps it is not used now."

"Oh, yes, it is," cried Nan. "Hark!" and she pushed back her sun-bonnet so that she could hear more distinctly.

Yes, surely it was a whistle, all three of the children heard it,—a long way off no doubt; but now they hear it again, and it sounded nearer.

"I think we ought to run down the track and stop the train," urged Rex.

"But how shall we do it?" Harry exclaimed. "I don't believe they would stop just for our calling; and besides, they might not hear us; we ought to signal somehow."

The words "signal somehow" suggested a red flag to Nan, for she knew that was what they used at times of danger, and the thought suggested—well, no matter what, but she disappeared behind a bush, and in a moment re-appeared, waving a veritable little red flag.

"Where did you get it?" cried the boys both at once, and staring at her in blank astonishment.

"It is my flannel skirt," Nan replied, with cheeks well nigh as scarlet as the skirt itself.

"Good for you, Nan; you're a 'cute one!" and Harry quickly fastened the skirt to the same stick with which he had poked the cow. Then he rushed off, calling, "Come on, Nan; but Rex had better wait here."

Harry gained a position upon the track from which his flag could be seen at a great distance.

Poor Rex! never had he felt so thoroughly out of patience with that lame leg of his. It seemed so hard not to be able to run with the best of them when there was so much excitement in the wind.

"May I go?" said Nan, appealingly, and as though she dared not stir without permission from his little Royal Highness.

"Of course, child," said the king, somewhat ungraciously.

Harry hurried along the track, and rounding the curve immediately gained a position, from which he knew the little flag could be seen from quite a distance? He reached the spot none too soon, for by this time the train was in sight. Right away he began waving vigorously. Nan's sun-bonnet was hanging from her neck, and she quickly untied the strings and shook it wildly up and down.

"Oh, Harry! do you think they see us?" she cried.

"See us! why, they can't help seeing us, goosie." Harry called Nan by this name more often than by any other. He did not mean it unkindly, and Nan did not mind.

"They are slowing up," cried Harry, jubilantly.

"They are slowing up," Nan repeated, in the vain hope that Rex might hear her. The next moment the train came to a standstill, and Nan dropped in a limp heap to the ground, for, trembling with excitement, her little limbs, stout though they were, refused longer to support her.

"Well, children, what's up?" shouted the engineer, from the cab of the locomotive. "I hope you ain't stopped the train for the fun of the thing."

"Well, I guess not," cried Harry, indignantly. "There's a dead cow on the track just round the curve; we were afraid she might throw your train off."

"Good for you," answered the man, "you may have saved us an ugly accident. Come, Joe," he called to the fireman, as he jumped from his engine. "Now show us where she is, Johnnie."

"My name's Harry," suggested that small gentleman, not caring to be addressed by the general title of Johnnie.

"Well, then, Master Harry, lead the way." Nan stayed where

she was. The excitement of the last few moments had robbed her of all strength; besides, she did not exactly want to see them drag that poor cow from the track. And now the people in the train began to crane their necks from the car windows to ascertain what might be the cause of the delay. A few men had gotten out and had gone ahead to investigate.

"What's wrong, honey?" asked an old woman of Nan, whose seat on the embankment brought her just on a level with the window.

"There's—there's a cow on the track," answered Nan, with a big sigh between the two "there's," as if her little heart had been quite overburdened.

"And de engineer saw it in time to stop de train? Tank de Lord!" ejaculated the old woman.

"No, no, he didn't; *we* stopped the train," Nan answered, proudly; "the engineer couldn't see the cow at all from here."

"Bress my heart! how did yer do it, chile?"

"Why, with my flannel skirt," Nan explained. She had not noticed that others in the car were listening to their conversation, but at this remark a coarse derisive laugh made her realise that a dozen pair of eyes were upon her. It proved too much for her overstrung nerves. She burst into tears and threw herself flat upon the grass, burying her face in her hands.

"Ye'd all oughter be ashamed o' ye'selves," said the old mammy, turning indignantly upon the fellow-passengers, though as much mystified as any of them by Nan's reply to her question.

Meanwhile the cow had been pulled from the track, and Regie and Harry were naturally much elated by the earnest commendation of the passengers who stood about them. "Look here," said one of them, evidently a farmer, "seems to me we ought to do something for these little people; who knows but some of us might have been in Kingdom Come but for them."

"That's so," answered another passenger, "but what can yer do more'n thank 'em? they look like gentlefolks' children. I reckon they wouldn't take money for doing a kind turn."

"Well, I guess not," said Regie, who had overheard the last remark.

"I thought so," answered the passenger, with a knowing wink. "He's got the right spirit, but I'd like to know one thing: where did you get that 'ere red flag?"

"It's my sister's flannel skirt," said Harry.

"And who was so awful 'cute as to think of it?"

"Why, Nan, of course," Harry replied, and as though Nan's "'cuteness" was a widely-accepted fact.

They had all been walking back toward the train as they talked, and now a warning whistle from the engineer hurried every one on board. As the wheels of the car began to turn slowly, the old mammy was the first to descry the little flannel skirt, whose mention had caused so much merriment, flying from the stick, which Harry had thrust into the ground when he had no farther use for it.

"Oh, see!" she cried, pointing towards it, "that's how she did it—she did make a flag of it. Now that's what I call 'cute.'"

"'Cute, I should say so," exclaimed the passenger who had been talking with Regie. "Let's give 'em three cheers as we go, one apiece, and the last and the loudest for the girl—the smart little owner of the little red skirt." At the sound of the hearty cheering Nan raised her head, with a smile shining through her tears. She had heard the old mammy's exclamation, and then she understood why the people had laughed when she told them she had stopped the train with her flannel skirt. How stupid of her not to have explained that she made a flag of it! Four slow puffs from the locomotive were heard above the cheering, then a dozen short quick ones, and in another second the train had rounded the curve and was out of sight, though for several minutes they could hear the noise of it growing fainter and fainter in the distance.

"Well, now we had better hurry home," said Rex, drawing a long breath. "It will be seven o'clock before we get there, and Sister Julia will be awfully worried."

Nan readjusted the little skirt that had done such good and novel service, and then they hurried back to Pet and the cart as fast as Regie could manage to get over the ground.

It was indeed nearly seven o'clock before they reached home, and Sister Julia *was* worried—worried enough to have been waiting at the gate an hour, peering up and down the road in the deepening twilight, wondering what could have happened, and which way they would come home, and sometimes wondering if they ever would come at all. Oh! how happy she felt when she recognised the patter of Pet's nimble feet on the hard boulevard, long before she could discover the little turnout itself.

"Bless your little hearts!" she cried, running to meet them, "I have been so worried! what has kept you such a long while?"

The children tried to tell all in one breath. "Oh, lots of things," they answered. "We had to wait to stop a train because a dead cow was on the track," said Nan.

"And Pet almost choked to death on a peach stone," added Rex, "and——"

"Oh, wait a moment," said Sister Julia, putting her fingers to her ears; "I cannot understand a word if you all talk at once."

Mrs. Murray was standing in the doorway; she had felt sure the children would come home all right. "How about the peaches?" she asked as they came up the path, for all this excitement did not make her forget that everything was in readiness for preserving the next day.

"Oh, they'll surely come to-night, the man promised faithfully," Harry answered. "Hark! I heard a waggon; I guess they're coming now." Yes, the waggon turned in at the gate, and Mrs. Murray's mind was as much relieved about the peaches as Sister Julia's about the children. The little trio did justice to an ample supper that night, and after an hour's narration of the exciting experiences of the day, they were perfectly willing to desert the open wood fire in the sitting-room for downy pillows and blankets, those comfortable contrivances which waft tired little people into the realm of slumberland.

IX.

A Day on the Beach

T had been arranged that for the first week Regie and Harry and Nan should be allowed to do pretty much as they liked, but after that lessons should be regularly begun with Sister Julia. Rex and Harry had reached about the same point in their studies, but poor little Nan was a good way behind, farther than her years would warrant. All the winter before she had attended school at the Branch, but she had pleaded very hard not to be sent back again.

"It is such a large school," she had told her mother, "that when you get ahead they have to hold you back for the other girls, and so you don't learn very much."

Mrs. Murray could not help smiling at her excuse for having made so little progress, knowing well enough the fault lay in the fact that she could not or would not apply her mind to the task which had been set her, but Nan hailed with delight this plan for studying with Sister Julia. Of course it had to be quite independently of the boys, because they were so far ahead of her, but somehow or other she was really in earnest about the matter, and did get along finely. The greatest incentive to hard study came to her in the mortification she felt one evening at not being able to enter into a game of Regie's, because she could not read the printing on the cards belonging to the game. Now that the children had settled down to their schooling the time flew faster than ever, and before they knew it, enough days had come and gone to allow "Uncle Sam," one morning, to shake a letter out of his mail-bag, directed to Regie and postmarked "London."

"See here, Reginald, I've brought something for you," called Captain Murray, coming with the mail, just as the children were setting off from the house, for it was Saturday and they had planned to spend the morning on the beach.

"Hurrah! here's another!" shouted Regie, for he had already received a steamer letter, which had been mailed when the *Alaska* touched at Queenstown.

"Yes, another letter," answered the captain, handing it to him, "and it's a rouser."

Regie stood irresolute a moment. "I tell you, boys," he said, always forgetting that Nan could not be included under this general title, "I tell you, I'll save it till we get fixed all comfortable on the beach, and then I'll read it to you."

"All right; let's start," said Harry, and the little party started, though Rex had some misgivings as to his ability to master Mamma Fairfax's handwriting, for he knew from the direction that the letter was from her. "We haven't played that king game much," he said, as they trudged along. He was able to manage with a little cane now in place of the crutches.

"Seems to me we're kind of playing it," answered Harry, glancing down at a heavy rug that he himself was carrying, and then over towards a luncheon basket with which Nan was laden: "at any rate the body-guard are sort of waiting on Your Highness."

"Arn't you ashamed of yourself, Harry Murray?" cried Nan, resenting the indignity. "You oughtn't to expect Regie to help carry things until he can walk as well as you and I do."

"I hope he'll walk a good sight better than you do before very long," retorted Harry, in a teasing mood. "See, Nan, this is the way you always get over the ground," and Harry threw aside the rug the better to imitate Nan's funny gait, characterised by a straightness on Nan's part amounting to an actual bending backward, and a jerky, independent little step. Harry hit it exactly, and Regie laughed immoderately, which was not very polite, considering Nan's gallant defence of him a few moments before. But Nan smiled, too, in spite of herself.

"I can't help it if I am too straight," she said; "there's one good thing,—straight people are not so dangerous of having consumption."

"Look out, Nan, you'll choke if you use such big words," advised Harry.

"No, really, I think it would be real fun to play the king game this morning," urged Regie, as they came to a spot on the beach where, by mutual consent, they spread out the rug and sat down.

"All right, then," replied Harry, "and I'll be the king."

"Then I shall not play," said Nan, "I am not going to keep changing kings every day."

"Of course not," Regie laughed, "you believe in the divine right, don't you, Nan?" Regie had just learned what "divine right" meant, and proudly aired his knowledge.

"I don't know," said Nan, "but whenever we play I believe in your being the king; I never could think of Harry as a king for a moment. Besides, you're our company, and we ought to wait on you."

"Bosh!" said Harry, "I don't call people what boards in your house, company."

"'What boards!'" repeated Nan. "Well, I should think you'd better brush up your grammar, Mr. Murray. Oh, the letter," she added, nodding in the direction of Regie's pocket.

"Oh, to be sure; why, I'd almost forgotten it," and Rex drew out his knife and carefully cut the envelope open at one end, after a neat little fashion of his own.

"'London, September 19th. My dear Reginald,'" he read, then paused, for in the very first sentence he discovered a word that he could not quite make out.

"Guess I'd better read it to myself first," he said, "there may be something private in it." Harry gave a significant cough, which meant that it was easy enough to see through such a flimsy excuse as that. Regie wisely paid no attention to it. Both the children knew it must necessarily be many minutes before they would be favoured with the contents of the letter, so Nan threw herself back on the rug, laid one arm under her head, and gazing out over the ocean gave herself up to the most delightful day-dreams. Harry resorted to whittling, that occupation of all leisure moments.

Suddenly, after ten minutes of unbroken quiet, Regie began again, making brief halts now and then before words that still proved a little puzzling.

"LONDON, *September* 19*th.*

"'MY DEAR REGINALD,—I doubt if there is a half hour in which we do not speak of you, or five minutes in that half hour in which we do not think of you, and so you can understand that we are pretty fond of a little fellow we have left behind us. Indeed, Papa Fairfax said, only a few minutes ago, that he wanted so much to see Regie that if he was not sure that he was very happy he thinks he would have to send some one away to America to bring him over.'"

"Oh! do you think he will?" questioned Nan.

"Of course not, goosie," Harry retorted, "don't interrupt again. Go on, Rex."

———"'But if he did,'" Regie resumed, "'you would have to hurry to catch us, for we shall be obliged to travel pretty fast as soon as we leave London. You do not need to get out the atlas to look up the place where this letter comes from, do you? Even little Nan knows how London looks on the map.'"

"Don't believe it," muttered Harry, half under his breath, but loudly enough for Nan to hear him.

"Do, too," whispered Nan, with a defiant shake of her curls; "but please don't interrupt. Go on, Rex." Rex did not mind these interruptions in the least, as they gave him a chance to look ahead a little.

"'It is ten years,'" he went on, reading slowly, "'since Papa Fairfax and I were here before, and we hardly know this London in the sunshine, for the old London of fog and rain, since we are having wonderfully clear weather. I shall have to wait till we reach home to tell you all about the sights of London. When you are older I shall hope to visit with you all the places where Papa Fairfax and I have been this morning,—Westminster Abbey, and St. Paul's, and the Tower. How you will enjoy the Tower, but in a sad sort of way, because so many sorrowful things have happened there. Last evening we strolled in for a while to see Madame Tussaud's wax figures, naturally looking rather more grimy and dusty than they did ten years ago.

"'And now, Rex, I have several other letters to send off by this same steamer, so this must do for the present. Do not forget to write once a week surely, either to Papa Fairfax or to me.

"'Yours lovingly,
"'MAMMA FAIRFAX.'"

"That's a nice letter," said Regie, gazing rather wistfully out to sea.

"Very nice," said Nan, "but you don't want to go, do you?"

Poor little Nan was blessed with a lively imagination. I say "poor Nan," for these lively imaginations play such sorry tricks upon the little folk and big folk who happen to possess them. Nan had but to catch a glimpse of the wistful look in Regie's eyes straightway to make up her mind that he was unhappy and lonely, and would gladly leave them all if he could.

"No, I don't want to go exactly," answered Rex; "but I guess you'd feel a little queer sometimes if that great ocean were between you and your father and mother."

"I do not believe I'd mind if I was on the same side of it with you, Regie," said Nan, betraying her unbounded admiration for his little Royal Highness.

"Nan, you're a regular spoony," remarked Harry.

"I don't know what a spoony is," Nan answered; "but of course it's something horrid, or you would not call me one," and she gave a little sigh which seemed to come almost from the soles of her boots. She did have to put up with a great deal of teasing from this brother of hers. Regie came to her rescue.

"You're not a spoony, Nan, at all," he said; "and, Harry, you don't deserve to have a sister. You do tease her awfully."

"What's the harm?" said Harry, sullenly. "But, Nan," he added, "I wish you would remember this, that I would not care to tease you if I did not really love you, and that when I stop it will be a bad sign."

"What's going on up there?" asked Nan, willing to change the subject.

"They're getting ready for a drill at the Life-saving Station," Harry answered, glancing in the direction toward which Nan was pointing. Regie was on the alert in a moment.

"Oh, are they? do let's go up there. I never saw a drill in all my life, and I never was in a Station but once."

It was an old story to Nan and Harry, but Regie was up and off, and the body-guard must needs follow.

The station was one of those low, oblong buildings, which,

dotting the coast at regular intervals, are to be found in the neighbourhood of all sea-shore resorts in the United States, and whose well-trained crew have been the means of saving many, many lives. This one little station at Moorlow had the grand record of having rescued five hundred persons in the nine years since it was established.

"What are you going to do?" asked Rex, the moment he came within speaking distance of two men who were dropping a coil of rope into a box.

"Going to have a drill," one of them answered; "there's no telling how soon we may have a wreck, and we must be ready for it. We had two last November."

Regie was about to say that he hoped they would have at least two this November, but realised what a dreadful wish that would be in time to check himself.

"What will be the best place to see it from?" he asked. "I would not miss any of it for the world."

The men were amused at his earnest manner.

"That boat hull will be a good place," said one of them; "but you'd better understand about things first. You see we are going to fire a shell out of this here howitzer, and the shell is fastened to this long coil of rope, so that when it goes whizzing away to the wreck it carries this rope—the whip-line we call it—with it."

"Yes, but where's your wreck?" Regie queried.

"Why, yonder," and the man pointed down the beach to where a piece of timber, with cross-pieces resembling a mast, was firmly planted in the sand. "There's our wreck, and we are going to send this rope flying over it."

"And what are you going to do then?"

"Why, then, one of the men, who is supposed to be on the wreck, will haul away on the line till the big rope which is fastened to the little rope is drawn over, so that we can send the breeches-buoy buzzing along the line."

"The breeches-buoy?" questioned Regie.

"Yes, to be sure. Have you never seen one?"

"I think not; I was never in a Life-saving Station but once, and that was in the summer, when there was nothing particular going on, and nobody to tell me anything."

"Then you come right along into the Station with me," said the man, kindly, "and I'll show you the breeches-buoy, and some other things besides. Why, there's Captain Murray's children," spying Harry and Nan seated on the sand at a little distance; "they know the old Station by heart. Hallo, Nan!" he called, "come, show this little stranger through the Station."

"Why, that's Reginald Fairfax, Mr. Burton," cried Nan,

coming toward them, and in a tone of surprise at such ignorance. "He lives at our house, and he's no little stranger at all."

"Oh, that's it, is it?" said Joe Burton, with elevated eyebrows; "well, then, Miss Murray, please have the kindness to show Mr. Fairfax through the Station."

Regie would have preferred to adhere to the original plan of having Mr. Burton for a guide, but was sufficiently polite not to betray his preference.

"You won't begin the drill before I come out, will you?" he called out to Mr. Burton.

"Never you fear," was the reassuring answer.

Nan showed Regie through, and was able to answer all questions to the perfect satisfaction of his little Royal Highness. First they went into the large room where the surf-boat was kept, and the life-saving car, which was oval in shape, with a cover fitting tightly over it. It was large enough to hold five people, and was sent out on the line to a wreck when the weather was too rough for the breeches-buoy. The breeches-buoy was a funny contrivance, made to accommodate one person at a time, and closely resembling a life-preserver in tarpaulin knee-breeches. Attached to it was an arrangement of pulleys and wheels, by means of which it could be run to and fro on a line from the wreck. At the farther end of the room hung the shells which had been fired from the mortar at different times. They were painted red, and each bore in white letters the name of the particular wreck to which it had proved such a welcome messenger.

From this larger room opened the "mess room," a kitchen, where the crew spent most of their time during the long winter months. A steep little stairway ran up from one corner to the loft overhead where the men slept. At one end of it a large window looked out to sea, and from the centre of the room a short flight of ladder-like stairs led into the cupola which surmounted the Station, and from which you see a great distance in every direction. The view from the cupola this clear October morning was glorious.

The water was wonderfully blue, with here and there a white sail skimming over it, as lightly and airily as the fleecy clouds across the blue of the sky. Regie and Nan stood side by side, taking in the beauty of the scene. Presently Nan said, "Yes, I do love the ocean so, it seems to me I couldn't live away from it; as though I should die if I had to, the same as little plants and things die without water."

"Yes, I guess you would," answered Regie; "and do you know, Nan, I believe you must have been born on just such a day as this, for your eyes have the same shade of blue in them as the sea. Besides, you are like a little wave anyway, a daring little wave that

comes scampering way up the beach and then—and then——,"
Rex paused. He was sure he had hold of a very fine idea, but
somehow he could not get on. A half-suppressed giggle from the
stairway did not help matters much, nor a whispered, "Guess
you're stuck, old fellow." Harry always had a faculty for turning
up when he was not wanted, and never when he was. Nan was
thoroughly provoked at him. She liked what Rex was saying
about her being just a little wave of the sea, and now she should
never know how he was going to finish. But for Rex Harry's

coming was quite fortunate, for he was himself quite at a loss to
know how he should wind up the flowery little speech begun so
bravely.

"You two spoonies had better come down," Harry added,
descending the little flight of stairs as noiselessly as he had come.
Just then one of the men waved his hand as a sign that the drill
was about to commence, and the children hurried down to join
Harry, where he sat comfortably established on the hull of the old
boat. The drill amounted to little more than a series of experi-

ments with the breeches-buoy. The whip-line was shot over the improvised mast, and one after another all the crew got into the buoy and came spinning down the line

"Oh! I should think that would be such fun," said Regie; "but unless we're wrecked some day I suppose we'll never have a chance to try it."

"Why not?" said Harry; "I warrant you they'll let us play with it awhile when the drill's over. I'll ask one of the crew."

"Seeing as you're Captain Murray's children we can't refuse you," answered Joe Burton, "but look out for yourselves, that you don't get a tumble. The little 'un had better not try it."

With Harry's help Rex managed to climb the ladder attached to the mast, and after they had each had two or three rides apiece, Nan could resist the temptation no longer. Watching her chance when the boys were standing for a moment with their backs turned, she clambered up the ladder, and dropped into the buoy. It was a very funny sight, the red-stockinged legs dangling in mid-air, and the blue eyes just peering over the edge of it, for she was such a little tot as to be quite swallowed up by this contrivance intended for grown-up people. But oh! the fun of it. It seemed more like flying than anything else in the world, and in regular turn Harry and Rex and Nan took ride after ride.

Never, I venture, did three children enjoy a morning of rarer sport, or do better justice to such a delicious dinner as they found waiting for them when they went home at noon.

X.

A Land Breeze.

DRIP! drip! drip! that was the sound that woke Sister Julia the next Saturday morning. It was the splash of water dropping from the eaves of the cottage on to the tin roof below. As soon as she heard it she gave a little half sigh, for what did it foretell but a rainy Saturday? and a rainy Saturday in that little cottage was likely to prove rather a sorry affair. In the first place it was a small cottage at any time, and doubly so on a rainy holiday, when three restless children must find their amusement within doors. In the second place, these three little people had a fashion of regarding a rainy Saturday as a sort of personal grievance, and accordingly indulged in considerable fretfulness.

On this particular morning Master Harry Murray hearing the ominous splashing, tumbled out of bed and flattened his gloomy little face against the pane.

"Is it raining?" called Nan, in a most woe-begone voice, from her bed in her own room.

"Raining? I should think so!" Harry called back. "It's

raining cats and dogs, and it is not going to stop for a minute all day. Besides, there's an awful fog. It's pretty hard lines, it strikes me, to study all the week with the sun shining bright, and then have it rain on your only holiday. I just wish I could have the managing of things in this old world for a while."

"I don't, then," called Nan; "it would be an awful hard world for girls. You wouldn't think of a thing but just what would please the boys."

Harry did not hear all of this, for he had flounced back into bed, drawing the blanket tight over his head, as though he meant to stay there for the rest of the day at any rate. Soon certain familiar odours, suggestive of a favourite breakfast, began to steal through his room, and his head gradually appeared above the covers, as though he were debating in his mind whether on the whole it would not be better to get up. A moment later the debate came to an end, for he heard his father's voice, and pricking up his ears it was easy enough to hear what he was saying.

"Look here, mother!" were the words that reached him, "the next time Harry is so late to breakfast he must go without it; I mean it, mother. The boy seems to be losing all regard for discipline. You can't manage a boy without discipline, no more'n a crew."

So it was not strange that Harry no longer questioned the advisability of getting up, but springing out of bed and dressing in a jiffy managed to put in an appearance at the table just as everyone else had finished. Mrs. Murray dropped some cakes on the griddle especially for him, and the lazy little fellow fared much better than he deserved. Mrs. Murray had a very soft spot in her heart for this only boy of hers, and Captain Murray's threat that another time Harry should go fasting set that soft spot to aching, and made her anxious to fortify him against such an emergency by heaping his plate high on this particular morning.

"Now I propose," said Sister Julia, after breakfast, when the children were moping and growling in the sitting-room, "that we have regular lessons to-day, and then you can take the first clear day as a holiday instead."

"No, sir-ree," answered Harry, decidedly. "You don't catch me studying on Saturday for nobody."

He felt rather ashamed of this speech as soon as it was uttered, but this was not a day when he was going to ask any one's pardon, not he—not even Sister Julia's, though he was very fond of her.

"You ought to be made to study every moment till you learn enough grammar to know that you ought never to use two negatives in one sentence," said Regie, indignant at the way in which Harry had spoken.

"What do you say to that proposition yourself, Regie?" asked Sister Julia.

"Well, to tell the truth, I don't feel much like it," said Regie; "my head aches a little."

"And mine aches like everything," and Nan threw herself on to the lounge and plunged her face into the sofa pillow, as though smothering itself were preferable to life on a rainy Saturday.

"Oh, dear me! what a disconsolate little trio," cried Sister Julia; "the wisest thing doubtless for me to do will be to take refuge in my own room and write some letters. When your troubles grow insupportable, come up, and we'll all try to be as miserable as possible together."

In their hearts that little trio must have felt very much ashamed of themselves, but they continued to mope and fret for another hour. By this time Mrs. Murray had gotten through with her morning work, and notwithstanding the rain, had gone in the buggy with Captain Murray to take some milk and fresh eggs to a sick woman down at the Branch.

"Oh, look here!" called Harry, wandering into the kitchen, and discovering that he was monarch of all he surveyed, "we've got everything to ourselves, we ought to have a regular good time, and do something unusual."

"Let's play tag through the doors," cried Nan, proposing a

game they were seldom allowed to indulge in because of the general disturbance and racket.

"No," said his little Royal Highness, in an authoritative way, "we'll have private theatricals. We'll act out a play," he added, when he saw by Nan's puzzled frown that she did not quite take in his idea.

"Good for you!" cried Harry, "that'll be the greatest fun. But oh! what do you suppose?" he exclaimed, suddenly lower-

ing his voice to an excited whisper,—"crouch! crouch down, both of you; this way, close to the window."

"What—what is it, Harry?" Nan asked, frightened at this strange performance, and regarding Harry in much the same dazed, sympathetic fashion as she had watched her little kitten endure the horrors of a fit the day before.

"Drop, drop, both of you!" was Harry's hoarse answer. "Don't you see? the Croxsons are coming."

Oh! that was it, the Croxsons were coming! Regie and Nan quickly obeyed Harry's order.

"How many of 'em?" asked Nan, from her prostrate position.

"The whole five," Harry answered, hopelessly; "but I don't believe they can see any of us, and if Sister Julia only does not hear them knock, and come down, they'll go away again and think no one's at home. Now, don't let's say a word."

There was the patter of two pairs of little feet without, and the scuffle of three pairs of others, and then there came a vigorous knocking at the kitchen door, again repeated after an interval of a few moments. The children held their breath.

"Guess they're all out," they heard Joe Croxson say, disconsolately.

"I think it's kind of mean to keep them out in the pouring rain," Nan whispered.

"And I know it is," answered Regie. "I say, let 'em in," and it was no sooner said than done.

Immediately the Croxsons crowded in after the manner of a rubber ball which may be forced through a very small aperture. They all contrived somehow or other to get through the door at once, but straightway spread out into so large a company that one could but wonder how they had managed it. None of them spoke a word till they were safely within doors, evidently deeming conversation of no importance in comparison with simply "getting in."

"We made up our minds you were all out," said Joe Croxson, at last, while the family were in the process of removing damp-smelling outer garments.

"We thought we'd fool you a while," Harry answered, with a nonchalant air.

The Croxsons were too glad to have gained entrance to take such treatment much to heart. "We've c-c-come to spend the morning, and stay to d-d-dinner, if you want us," said little Madge, who stuttered dreadfully.

'I'm pretty sure it won't be convenient to have you stay to dinner," said Nan, who no sooner beheld the shabby little Croxsons disposing themselves about the room with a permanent air, than with charming inconsistency she straightway regretted her noble impulse to let them all in. That they were a shabby little company no one could for a moment deny. The three girls, the youngest little more than a baby, each wore a ragged dress, and for an out-of-door wrap a faded and colourless strip, which collectively had once formed a shawl of their mother's.

The mother herself had died five years ago, and since then the children had managed for themselves as best they could. Their father was fireman on one of the engines belonging to the local road that ran through Moorlow, and the children were alone from morning till night. A poor woman came in every morning to cook their oatmeal and "tidy up," but being poorly paid, the tidying up was always hasty, and never thorough. They were rather a stupid-looking set of children, and no wonder! You would hardly expect to find much that was bright in their faces, with so little brightness in their lives; besides, none of them had ever been to school, and Joe, who was the oldest of them all, knew little more than his letters, although he had passed his eleventh birthday. Everyone felt sorry for the Croxsons; and no doubt they would have fared better in one of the large cities, where they would have been reached by some of the organised charities, than in a little place like Moorlow. The rich people, who came in the summer in search of rest and refreshment, did not interest themselves in the villagers, and the villagers themselves were mostly hard-working fishermen with little time or money to devote to others. Had it not been for the Murrays the Croxsons would surely have fared much worse. Mrs. Murray did them many a kind turn, and when Madge had a fever the winter before, Harry or Nan had trudged backward and forward every day with beef tea or some other nourishing food. So there was one bright spot in their lives after all. Indeed, there was more than one, for born by the sea they loved it dearly, and in warm sunshiny weather they romped on the beach the whole day long, keenly enjoying their perfect freedom, and pitying the children obliged to go to school. Nan always spoke of them as the "poor little Croxsons," and it was this pathetic side of their history which made her second Regie's motion to open the door.

"Of course we can't play that game now, and all our fun is spoiled," said Harry, seeming to utterly disregard the feelings of the Croxsons. Fortunately they were not sensitive, and their stolid little faces showed no signs either of pain or resentment.

"Oh, yes, we can," answered Regie; "they'll be the audience."

"The very thing!" cried Nan, enthusiastically. "Now, children," turning to the Croxsons, "we are going to have a play, and you'll be the audience, won't you?"

Each little Croxson nodded in the affirmative, though they had

not the remotest idea what it was they were to be. They were literally clay in the hands of the potter when they were at the Murrays'. They did not care what was done with them, or to them, so long as they were simply allowed to stay. Harry fancied the idea of an audience, and preparations were at once begun. The clothes-horse was converted into scenery by covering it with a green plaid blanket-shawl, the ironing table was pressed into service as a settee for the audience, and the five Croxsons were packed into it in one tightly wedged row. From the commencement of the performance to its tragic end they sat staring in open-eyed astonishment; for they had never seen anything like it before—nor had any one else, for that matter. The plot of the play beggars description. Suffice it to say that Nan figured as the heroine, with a blue gingham apron for a train and a dish towel for a turban. Harry, muffled in a red table cover, was terrible as a sort of border ruffian, and Regie played the part of Nan's gallant brother. In a greater part of the performance there was so much action, so much rushing on and off the stage, that it was difficult to gain a clear idea of what was really intended; but matters culminated in a hand-to-hand scuffle between Harry and Reginald—a wooden spoon and a toasting fork doing service as weapons. Finally

Harry succumbed, and fell to the ground with the rather inelegant exclamation, "Stabbed! stabbed to the liver!" and Nan falling in a swoon to the floor was enveloped in the green plaid shawl, which she accidentally pulled down with her.

"Oh, Harry! why did you give out?" cried Joe Croxson, never more excited in his life.

"It was planned for me to die," Harry answered, still lying motionless on the floor. "I was Regie's sister's lover, and I'm a fraud and a wretch."

The play had lasted almost an hour, and to the great delight of all concerned.

"P-p-please d-d-do it again!" begged little Madge. Rex and Nan were in favour of a repetition, but for Harry the novelty was gone, and novelty was everything with him.

"No, I've had enough," he said, decidedly, and so the project had to be abandoned. Meanwhile Harry's assertion that it was going to rain all day was fast being contradicted, for it had stopped raining, and now and then the sun shone out bravely through a rift in the clouds. With the sunshine came a distaste for indoor fun, and there was a rush for hats and coats preparatory to a rush out into the November air. Nan, with tender thoughtfulness, had hung the Croxsons' wraps on chairs near the fire, and now they were dry, and as fit for use again as it was possible for such sorry clothes to be. At last all were ready, and Regie hurrying to open the door that led to the porch from the kitchen, found it locked and the key gone. The little party stared at each other. Harry was missing, and nowhere to be seen. Of course he was the guilty one. Then there was a stampede for the sitting-room door. Locked, too, and minus the key. A suppressed titter from the head of the stairs made them all look up.

"Why don't you go out?" Harry giggled; "I'd be ashamed if I couldn't open a door."

"Come down and give us those keys this minute," demanded Nan, in a tone most unlikely to accomplish her object. Harry only smiled provokingly. All in vain the children begged and coaxed. Finally they scrambled up the stairs to gain possession of them by main force if possible. Meanwhile Nan, evolving a little scheme out of her own head, slipped into Harry's room, appearing again in a trice with his Sunday suit in her hand. Harry had great regard for that Sunday suit, and Nan knew it.

"Look here, Harry!" she cried, "I will throw this downstairs if you don't give up those keys right away."

"You dare!" called Harry, still engaged in a scuffle with the boys, "and I know what I'll do."

Alas! Nan dared, and the precious suit fell in a crumpled mass to the floor below. By a sudden jerk Harry freed himself from his captors, and rushing into Nan's room, dragged pillow and bed-clothes from the bed, and then pitched them over the banisters. In a second they were followed by bolster and mattress. The little Croxsons and Regie looked on in speechless astonishment The general encounter had reduced itself to single combat between Harry and Nan.

"Well!" said Nan, "mother will soon be home, and then we'll see what will happen. Harry Preston Murray" (Nan always called Harry by his full name when out of patience with him), "you have an awful temper!"

'I'll teach you not to touch my clothes again, any way," Harry answered, carefully shaking and folding the precious trousers.

"But you don't know when to stop, Harry," sighed Nan, coming down the stairs and surveying the havoc wrought with real dismay. What would her mother say and do about it? Harry began to have some misgivings of his own on the subject.

"You will have to carry all those things up again," she said, in a half-pleading tone.

"And I'll help you, though you ought to be made to do it all yourself," added Regie.

Harry came to the conclusion that he *would* have to carry them up again sooner or later, and deemed it wise to commence before any one arrived on the scene. Besides, there was an ominous sound of wheels down the road. It might be Captain and Mrs. Murray. Joe Croxson had his own fears regarding this possibility, and beckoning his brothers and sisters into a corner, confided to them that he thought they had better take their departure. "There's going to be a row," he whispered, "when the old 'uns come home. Harry 'll catch it, and if we don't look out we'll catch it too." To the little Croxsons a hint was sufficient. Owing to certain personal experiences of a painful character, they seemed to live in a constant dread of what they termed "catching it." The keys had fallen from Harry's pocket in the confusion, and hurriedly unlocking the door, the whole five slipped out and stole noiselessly away, without so much as saying "by your leave," or "good-bye," either to host or hostess. Harry and Rex and Nan, toiling, tugging, and shoving the unwieldy mattress upstairs, did not miss them till many minutes afterward. Indeed, they were each too much absorbed with their own thoughts to notice anything. Regie was the only one who saw any funny side to the proceeding, and the corners of his mouth twitched a little. Nan was on the verge of actual tears. The sight of her dainty little pillow shams and coverlid so sadly rumpled was almost too much for her. Harry was indignant over having to undo his own mischief, and did everything in a jerky, disagreeable way. Finally the little bed was in some sort of order, but as Nan was adjusting the pillow, Harry, giving her a shove which sent her into the middle of the bed, exclaimed, "You are enough to try the patience of a saint, Nan!"

It needed nothing more to bring Nan's threatening tears to the surface, and lying just where Harry had pushed her, she burst into sobs and tears. If there was one thing Harry hated more than another it was to have Nan cry, and to add to his discomfort Sister Julia came hurrying into the room. She had heard the romping in the hall, but never dreamed that it needed investigation till Nan's crying reached her.

"Why, what is the matter?" she questioned.

"There's a great deal the matter," Regie replied, calmly; "and I should think Harry would be ashamed of himself."

"Nan began it," said Harry, with Adam-like self-excusing.

"Harry got so mad," explained Regie, excitedly, "that he threw——".

"Wait a minute, Regie, let Harry tell me himself."

"Yes, I got so mad," said Harry, using Regie's own words, "that I took everything from Nan's bed and pitched it downstairs. Nan threw my Sunday suit down first, or I would never have thought of it. But I helped bring all the clothes up again, so I don't see what she wants to cry about it now for."

"I am not crying about that at all, Sister Julia," sobbed Nan, without raising her head; "I'm crying because he said 'I was enough to try the patience of a saint.' I don't know what it means, but I think it's an awful unkind thing for a brother to say."

Sister Julia could hardly keep from smiling at this unexpected turn of affairs. Harry and Regie laughed outright, which did not help matters much.

Sister Julia motioned the boys from the room, and sitting down by Nan, on the side of the bed, stroked the brown curls till the sobs grew few and far between. Then she explained that "she was enough to try the patience of a saint" was not such a very dreadful thing for Harry to have said, and finally induced Nan to admit, smiling through her tears, that both she and Harry were to blame, and that on the whole they had had rather a funny time of it. Presently Captain and Mrs. Murray came home, finding everything in order about the house. Only you and Sister Julia, little reader, ever heard the full history of that rainy Saturday morning.

XI.

A New Friend

T was early in November, but if you had lain by Nan's side on the beach basking in the sunshine you would scarcely have guessed it. The air was mild and warm, and there were no trees near to betray what sad havoc blustering fall winds had made with the foliage. Old ocean was as blue and still as in midsummer, with just a single line of breakers falling at regular intervals on the hard white beach. Nan was fairly glorying in the June-like day, feeling there could hardly be such another till June herself should have come round again. The boys had gone off for the afternoon on some sort of an expedition, never so much as asking her to accompany them, but she was not sorry to be left at home. She was one of those little people who, like some big people, loved to have a chance for a quiet think now and then, and lying there by herself she was supremely happy and tranquil. She had been there fully an hour, and for a while had been busy building a little castle in the sand, making a foundation of clam shells, and using an old bottle for a tower.

Most of the time she had been "just thinking," and thinking so hard that she did not notice some one coming nearer and nearer until, suddenly looking up, her eyes met those of a stranger. She was a pretty little picture lying there flat on the sand, with her dimpled face propped comfortably between her hands.

"I wonder what you are thinking about, my little friend," said the new comer, kindly. "I know from your face that your thoughts are happy thoughts?"

"Pretty foolish ones, I guess you'd call them!" laughed Nan,

for there was something about the stranger that at once won her confidence.

"I'm not so sure of that," he answered; "but a stranger has no right to ask you what they were, so good-bye, my little dreamer."

"I wish you would not go," said Nan, sitting up and smoothing out her dress; "I would like to talk to you, because I think you look like a minister, and I never spoke to a real minister before."

"Well, you shall now," he answered, sitting down beside her, "for you have guessed rightly, and for that matter there is nothing the minister would rather do than talk to you for a while."

There was a little pause, and then Nan asked hesitatingly, as though she feared to seem rude, "You don't belong about here, do you?"

"No, but I almost wish I did. I love the sea with all my heart, so that I have hard work to keep from saying something about it in every sermon I preach. But if I do not belong about here, it is very certain that you do. You must have lived by the ocean week in and week out, to get that shade of blue into your eyes."

"That's what Reginald says!" laughed Nan.

"And who is Reginald?"

"Why, Reginald Fairfax; he's staying with us while his father and mother are in Europe. The poor little fellow broke his leg last summer, and Sister Julia is here too, to take care of him, but he's almost well now. I wish you knew Sister Julia. She comes from one of the great hospitals in New York, and she is the loveliest person you ever saw."

"Well, I should say I did know her," answered the minister. "She goes to my church in town, and so do Mr. and Mrs. Fairfax; and Regie and I are the best of friends."

"Why, are you Mr. Vale?" queried Nan, astonished, for the name of the young minister had often been on Regie's lips.

"Yes, I am," he answered, laughing, as though he must own up to the truth.

"But what are you doing here?"

"Well, I'll tell you. Do you see that red-tiled cottage yonder?" pointing down the beach.

"Do you mean Mr. Avery's?" for Nan knew the name of every resident in the neighbourhood of Moorlow.

"Yes; Mr. Avery is a friend of mine, and stays down here, you know, quite late into the fall, so he asked me to bring my sister, who is quite an invalid, to his cottage, thinking the change would do her good. So here we are; we came this morning, but I am obliged to go back to the city again this afternoon."

"Oh, dear! I'm sorry for that," said Nan, regretfully, "I would so much have liked to hear you preach."

"Well, that is very kind of you. Perhaps you can some time, when you come to New York to visit Regie. By the way, where is he?"

"Oh, he's off with my brother Harry this afternoon, and I don't believe they'll be home before supper time."

"That's too bad, but I shall probably see him the next time I come."

"Oh, you are coming again then!" exclaimed Nan, her face brightening.

"Yes, surely. Once a week, at least, so long as my sister stays. And now, suppose you tell me something about yourself. Your name is———"

"Nannie—Nannie Murray," answered Nan.

"And you live———"

"In that brown cottage behind us there on the bluff," nodding her head in the direction of the house.

"And you have lived there always?"

"Yes, sir," she replied, proudly.

"Then you are a fortunate little maiden. To have grown up by the sea is something to be very thankful for. It seems a pity to live in town when one loves the sea and open country as much as I do."

"Why don't you come down here?" urged Nan. "There are plenty of houses."

"But the bother of it is there are plenty of people in town, and the preacher must stay near the people. It is more beautiful and wonderful, you know, to be able to help a soul struggle up toward high-water mark, than even to watch the tide come in as we are doing. But I think I must be talking quite over your head. Now that we are friends, perhaps you will not mind telling me what you were thinking about when I so rudely interrupted you?"

"Do you see that schooner, away off there?" Nan answered. "Well, when you came it was right in front of me, and I was pretending it was sailing away to a beautiful island with a crowd of poor city children on board, who had never been very well, or had a very happy time, and I pretended they were already beginning to look fresh and rosy with the salt breeze blowing in their faces; and I made believe that some of the children had a glass, and were looking here at me on the beach, and that some of them thought I was a mermaid, and others a queer sort of a fish. Now I suppose you think those were pretty foolish thoughts, don't you?"

"Not a bit of it. It is like a fairy story, only better. But before you began to build a castle in the air, I see you built a little one here in the sand. I suppose you have peopled this with a lot of queer little people of your own too."

"No," said Nan, honestly, "I don't make up things much, except when I am just looking out to sea."

"Have you ever thought, Nan," said Mr. Vale, earnestly, as he banked up a falling wall of her castle with his hand, "that your own life is a sort of little castle, wonderfully made, richly furnished, beautiful and hopeful to look upon? It is fitting that only One should live in that fair house—He who is purity and goodness and truth Himself. Ask Him to come and dwell within you, to look out of your eyes, to hear with your ears, to speak through your lips, to guide your hands and your feet."

"You mean Jesus, don't you?" asked Nan, looking frankly into his face with sweet simplicity.

"Yes, my little friend, I do."

"Well, it is just like a sermon."

"But you said, you know, that you would like to hear me preach."

"Yes, I did," answered Nan, thoughtfully, gathering up a handful of sand and letting it sift through her fingers, "and I like your preaching; I like it very much indeed."

"Thank you," and Mr. Vale looked as though he deeply appreciated Nan's honest praise; "but it is high time the preacher was off. There is the train whistle now! give my love to Regie, and I shall surely run over to see him next week when I come down."

Nan watched her new friend hurrying away to the station, and stood transfixed till a low sand-hill hid him from sight. Then she scampered to the house to tell of her good fortune.

As soon as Regie came home, and while he was making a hurried toilet for supper, Nan ran into his room, and curling herself up on the window-box, commenced, for the third time (for Sister Julia and Mrs. Murray had already been favoured), to give an excited narration of the afternoon's experiences.

"Oh, Regie!" she began, "I've had the most splendid time— a good long chat with a real live minister. He came from the city, and he told me the nicest things, sort of preached, you know; and he loves the sea just as much as I do, and his sister is staying up at the Averys', so he's coming again. He's a young minister, Regie, and he has the loveliest face."

"I don't like men with lovely faces," said Regie, scornfully.

"Well, you'd like his face, Regie. It was like a great strong angel's face, and he told me he knew you, and for me to give you his love, and to tell you that when he came again he would surely come and see——"

"You don't mean Mr. Vale, do you?" cried Regie

"That's just who I do mean," Nan answered, complacently.

"Oh, dear me! why wasn't I round? Are you sure he's coming again?"

"Sure," said Nan, wondering if it was selfish to be glad that just this once Regie had not been "round" at all, and that she had the young clergyman quite to herself.

XII.

The "Starling" runs ashore.

ERTAIN unmistakable signs were in the wind by which anyone could have told that Thanksgiving Day was comparatively close at hand. There was a vigorous stoning of raisins on the part of Mrs. Murray, an odour of cider in the air which pointed plainly to the concoction of mincemeat, and Nan was confident she detected the largest turkey scratching round the yard in a nervous, timorous sort of way, as though he knew his days were numbered. By the calendar the eventful occasion was still ten days off, when one cold and blustering afternoon Captain Murray came home from the Life-saving Station, and into the cosy kitchen.

"If I'm not very much mistaken," he said (and in the matter of weather Captain Murray seldom was mistaken), "we are in for a pretty heavy storm. We shall need to be on the look out, every man of us at the Station, the whole night through. Give us a hearty supper, Mollie, that'll keep a fellow well braced till morning."

"Do I ever put you off with a poor supper, Epher?" asked Mrs. Murray, reproachfully, pausing a moment in her mixing of some gingerbread in a large yellow bowl.

"Never with a poor supper, mother, only you know what I mean. Give us sort of an extra touch to-night."

THE "STARLING" RUNS ASHORE.

Mrs. Murray knew as well as could be what her good husband meant by "an extra touch," and soon the waffle-iron was taken from its hook and Harry was on his way to the cellar to fill the maple syrup cup. It was one of those nights when a cosy, comfortable home seems doubly comfortable and cosy, and very reluctantly Captain Murray put on his great coat to go back to the Station as soon as supper was over. The rain was falling

in torrents now, and as he opened the sitting-room door, a gust of wind whipped in, sending the papers on the table whirling to the floor and overturning the lamp, which fortunately went out as it fell. When order was again restored, Sister Julia began reading a bright little story aloud to the children by way of cheering them up a bit. Even Harry was quite overawed by the violence of the storm, for by this time it was violent. The wind was blowing a gale now, and it had grown so cold that the fire had to be constantly replenished to keep the room comfortably warm. At nine o'clock the children went upstairs, and were glad enough to hurry into bed, for on such a night as this it was impossible to heat the upper story of the little cottage.

"I'm glad there's a great big lighthouse at the Highlands," Regie called out after he had gotten into bed.

"So am I," answered both Nan and Harry, and with this comforting thought in mind they all fell asleep. But Sister Julia and Mrs. Murray scarcely closed their eyes the whole night long. Sometimes it seemed as though the little cottage could not hold its own against such a terrific blow. At daybreak Mrs. Murray came up to Sister Julia's room, to find her already dressed.

"I think there's something wrong at the Station," she said. "Hereward and Ned have been barking and bounding about in the most excited fashion for the last half-hour. Then, when the wind dies down for a second, I think I can hear the voices of the men calling to each other."

"Yes, and look here," answered Sister Julia, pressing her white face close to the pane; "I imagine I can discover the masts of a schooner near the beach."

"Yes, surely; there must have been a wreck," and Mrs. Murray threw open the window to see more clearly. "Hark!" she added, "now don't you hear the men?"

"Of course I do," cried Sister Julia; "and I can stand it no longer. I must bundle up and go down and see for myself."

"Oh! my child, you ought never to go," exclaimed Mrs. Murray, but at the same time she helped her to hurry into her heavy ulster. "Oh, dear! I've a good mind to go with you; but no, it will not do to leave the children. Send one of the men up though, as soon as possible, to let me know what has happened, and that you have reached the Station without being blown away."

So out into the storm went Sister Julia, and Hereward and Ned were at her side in an instant. The rain had ceased falling, but the wind still blew a hurricane, and in walking from the cottage to the station all her strength was needed to bear up against it. She had gone but a little way before she discovered that a schooner *had* run ashore, and she tried to quicken her steps, fearing and yet anxious to know the truth. Just here I would tell my young reader that this story, so far as it relates to the work done that morning by the Life-saving crew, is every word true. Somebody, whom I choose to call Captain Murray, could show you a letter, sent, in company with a gold medal, from the Government at Washington, and written in appreciation of his gallant services and those of his brave crew, and in which

you could read a graphic narration of all that happened that eventful November morning.

As Sister Julia neared the Station she heard the men shouting to each other in such cheery tones that she felt sure no lives could have been lost, and her heart grew lighter. The crew were at some sort of work down on the beach, and unnoticed by anyone she entered the Station from the landward side. The large room was empty, but the door stood open into the kitchen, and there what a strange sight met her eyes! Four men were huddled round the stove trying to get a little warmth into their half-frozen bodies. On one blanket on the floor, covered by another, lay a poor woman, who looked half-dead; and seated on a stool near her was Captain Murray, endeavouring to remove the dripping clothing from a screaming baby lying across his knees.

"God bless you!" he exclaimed, looking up and discovering Sister Julia, "you've come in the nick of time. We've just brought these poor wretches in from the wreck yonder, and I've sent Burton up to the house to get some dry duds for the woman and this baby," and he laid the soaking little specimen of humanity in Sister Julia's arms.

"Now, my hearties," he said cheerily, turning to the men, "hurry up to the loft, strip off your wet clothing, wrap yourselves in the blankets you'll find there, and turn into the bunks. You'll have to stay there till your clothes are dry, but I reckon you're tired enough to be willing to. We'll get you up some breakfast as soon as possible. Now I'm off," he added, turning to Sister Julia. "I am needed on the beach more than here."

The shivering little company about the stove promptly and gladly obeyed Captain Murray's orders, and Sister Julia, having succeeded in quieting the baby, began to remove its draggled clothing. Just then someone came in from the large room.

"There were no lives lost, were there?" she asked, eagerly, without looking up, presuming it to be one of Captain Murray's crew, and in the same instant the newcomer asked the same question of her.

"No, no lives lost," answered the woman on the floor, in a weak, exhausted voice. The new comer was Mr. Vale, who had come down to Moorlow the night before, and Sister Julia was glad enough to welcome him, for she needed someone to aid her.

"My poor woman, you ought to get that wet clothing off at once," said Mr. Vale, bending over her.

"I know it, sir, but I'm that weak."

"I can attend to her now, if you'll take the baby," said Sister Julia.

"With the greatest of pleasure," and Mr. Vale took the

blanketed baby into his arms, with a knack that showed his love for children. Straightway he went up aloft, with the little stranger gazing comfortably over his shoulder, to enquire for the welfare of the men. No sooner had he gone than Burton came hurrying in with the bundle of clothing which Mrs. Murray had gotten together. Quickly and skilfully Sister Julia helped the woman to make the change, and had but just finished buttoning a warm flannel wrapper about her when, overcome by fatigue, she fell asleep in the chair in which she was sitting.

"These good people had better have something to eat as soon as possible," said Mr. Vale, returning down the narrow stairway, "and if you can show me a place to put this baby, for it is fast asleep, we'll see about getting some food ready for them."

"Here's a good place for it," and Sister Julia let down a wide shelf that was fastened against the wall, and with her ulster rolled up for a pillow, made the little waif very comfortable, for it was too young a baby to be in danger of rolling off. Captain Murray put his head in at the door just then with a most anxious face.

"It is raining," he said, "and the storm is increasing every moment. I can't spare one of the men, for we must lose no time in getting the life-saving tackle in order, though it is not probable we shall need to make use of it twice in one morning. Do you think you can manage to get a breakfast together, Sister Julia?"

"Aye, aye, sir," answered Mr. Vale, cheerily, "we'll attend to that."

"That must be Nan's new friend," thought Captain Murray, but he could not take the time to find out, and hurried away, feeling that he had left his shipwrecked party in good hands. Then Mr. Vale and Sister Julia set right away to work to investigate the supply of provisions in the Station. Mr. Vale peered into boxes, and Sister Julia lifted covers of crocks and dishes, and then they looked at each other rather blankly, for they were disappointed at the result.

"I have it," said Sister Julia, after a moment's thought. "The best thing, I think, would be for you to put on your coat and make your way as best you can to Mrs. Murray's. She will have the oatmeal on the fire by this time," glancing at the clock on the high shelf overhead, " and it would be just like her, remembering the hard work going on down here, to have made a larger quantity than usual."

Mr. Vale was off in a moment, and then Sister Julia made preparations for boiling the coffee, carrying the coffee-mill into the larger room, so as not to wake the baby and its mother with the clatter of the grinding. Afterward she set the little table as best she could, and slicing some stale bread she had found in the closet, placed it at one side ready for toasting. So she busied herself about one thing and another till there was nothing more to be done. It seemed to her as though Mr. Vale would never come back, but in a really marvellously short space of time there was a tramping outside the door, and in came a little party, well laden with tin pails and baskets. They were all there—Mrs. Murray and Nan, Reginald and Harry; and indeed all were needed, to carry safely through such a storm as that the generous breakfast which Mrs. Murray had prepared; and the whole family at once set about serving it. The children trudged up and down the steep stairway, carrying the steaming coffee and oatmeal to the men in the loft.

"Bless your little heart!" said one of the men, as he took a brimming cup from Nan's hand; but the others seemed too hungry to take time to say so much as "thank you." Sister Julia woke the tired mother, who fell asleep again as soon as she had eaten a little, and then she quieted the baby, who had begun to cry lustily, with a breakfast of warmed milk served in a ginger-ale bottle. As soon as she could be spared, Mrs. Murray put on her cloak and hurried down to the beach to see how that good captain of hers was enduring all this excitement and fatigue. For the captain, as he himself said, "was not so young as he once was," and could not stand up as well as in other days against wind and weather.

"Oh, Mollie!" he called, as soon as she came near enough for his voice to reach her, "go back to the Station; you'll catch your death o' cold in this driving wind."

THE "STARLING" RUNS ASHORE.

"No fears for me, Epher," she called back, "but you must go right up to the Station yourself, you and the men, and get some breakfast, or you'll be down sick, every one of you."

All hands were only too glad to obey this order, for the life-

saving apparatus was again intact, and they were very hungry. Filing into the big room, they laid aside their tarpaulins, and then sat down to a better breakfast than ever before graced their mess table. It did Mrs. Murray's heart good to see how thoroughly they enjoyed it, and when the captain said, "I'd like to see the wife that can compare with Mollie Murray," the colour flushed proudly into her face.

It was eight o'clock when the hungry party finished breakfast, and they were just pushing their chairs back from the table when one of their crew, who had been left on the beach on patrol duty, threw open the door and called for aid.

"Can it be possible that we are to have another wreck this morning?" thought the captain, as he and his men hurried into their tarpaulins, and rushed out of the Station. But alas! it was possible, for a short distance up the beach another vessel was stranded. In a moment the little house was quite deserted. Calling for their clothes, the men who had been rescued from the *Starling* got into them, wet as they were, and, accompanied by Mr. Vale, hastened to render what service they could. Notwithstanding the commotion the mother and baby still slept quietly on in the kitchen, while Sister Julia, Mrs. Murray, and the children crowded into the seaward window of the loft, to watch as best they could the terribly exciting scene taking place below them on the beach.

XIII.

The Wreck of the Spanish Brig.

THE storm that culminated on that November morning was the worst that had been known on the Moorlow coast for years. The wind, which was north-east, blew a hurricane averaging eighty-four miles an hour. The beach was flooded by a furious surf, and, strangely enough for that time of the year, the weather was freezing cold. In less than ten minutes after the second vessel stranded Captain Murray's crew was abreast of her, but in the meantime she had worked to within a hundred yards of the beach, and Joe Burton, running down behind a receding wave, cast a line on board with a vigorous throw of the heaving-stick.

"Hurrah for Burton!" cried Harry. "He's a fine fellow, I tell you."

As soon as the line reached the ship, the sailors on board of her tugged away at it until they had pulled up the larger line, on which Captain Murray purposed to send out the breeches-buoy. But before the buoy could be rigged up, the sailors, ignorant of

Joe Burton, running down behind a receding wave, cast a line on board with a vigorous throw of the heaving-stick.

his purpose, showed that they were going to endeavour to reach the land by coming hand-over-hand along the rope. Captain Murray and his men shouted from the shore, and wildly gesticulated, for it seemed impossible that any of them could reach the shore alive in that way. The surf was very violent, but the greatest danger lay in the fact that the position of the brig in the set of the strong current caused an enormous swirl of water between her and the beach, which retained eddying masses of wreckage, mainly cord-wood from the wreck of the *Starling*, and which masses were continually swept out by the undertow, and hurled in by the breakers.

"Oh, those foolish men! those foolish men! why don't they understand and see their danger?" cried Sister Julia, attempting to draw the children away from a sight so distressing; but the boys were immovable. Mrs. Murray, Sister Julia, and Nan went down to the little kitchen to wait, since they no longer had the heart to watch.

"There, one of the fellows has started!" cried Harry, with long pauses between his sentences, "and he's all right so far. No; my goodness, there he goes! a wave has flung him over the rope, and his head is caught between the cords of the whip-line. He will choke to death. No! there goes Burton again right into the surf holding on to the line. There! he's got him, he's got the sailor; but how can he ever bring him to land? See, Rex, he's clinging to a piece of driftwood with one hand, and holding on to the sailor with the other."

"Oh! but another man is trying it now!" exclaimed Rex. "Oh! why don't they wait? Look there—and another one of the crew has plunged in after him; but, goodness! the driftwood has knocked him completely under. Ah! there go two more of the men in to his rescue, and Burton is in the breakers again, too. Who's that with him, Harry?"

"I can't make out, but—hurrah! they've reached the sailor; they'll save him, I know."

And Harry was right; they did save him, and five others besides, all of whom attempted the same foolhardy method of reaching the land, and all of whom were rescued by the same hand-to-hand struggle in the surf on the part of Captain Murray's gallant crew.

"I never saw such bravery, never!" called Mr. Vale, and it could plainly be seen that his enthusiasm cheered the men

wonderfully in their perilous work. He longed to plunge in with them, but he knew that he would be powerless to render any aid. It was their long experience that was standing the crew in such good stead. By this time a crowd had gathered on the beach, that is, every able-bodied resident of Moorlow was there, and as the last sailor was brought safely to shore a hearty cheer went up that, for the moment, even rose above the pounding of the breakers on the shore. Stretched on the sand, in such shelter from the wind and rain as the side of the surf-boat afforded, the disabled seamen were laid. They were all Spaniards, and only two of them were able to stand upon their feet.

"Which of you is captain of the brig?" asked Captain Murray, looking kindly down upon this second group of shipwrecked mariners.

"He no here," answered one of them who had been the least hurt, in broken English; "when he think his ship go to pieces, he go below and make hisself dead;" but the man's gestures told more plainly than his words that the captain had shot himself in the head.

Captain Murray turned to his men with a look that meant, "Our work is not over yet."

"What shall be done with these poor fellows?" ventured Mr. Vale, when he saw that the thought of how he should reach the man still on the brig had driven all other thoughts from the captain's mind.

"Lord knows!" answered Captain Murray, sorely puzzled. "It'll be more'n a week before some of them will get out of bed, when they once get into it. There's some ugly bruises among 'em."

"Do you think we could make them comfortable in the chapel on the beach yonder? It would serve splendidly for a hospital."

"The very thing! I'll leave the arrangements to you, sir," said Captain Murray, confident now that this really was Nan's new friend, the minister, about whom she had talked so much.

The first thing to be done was to get the exhausted Spaniards up to the Station, where Rex and Harry and Nan, with excited, earnest faces, waited to receive them. Over and over again the children had begged and entreated to be allowed to run down to the scene of the wreck, but Mrs. Murray had thought best to refuse them.

Captain Murray could not have left the preparation of the

116   *HIS LITTLE ROYAL HIGHNESS.*

hospital in better hands than Mr. Vale's. Won by his handsome face and simple manner, the villagers crowded about him, eager to do his bidding. The sexton of the little church hurried home for the keys as fast as his rheumatic old limbs could carry him, and with the aid of Joe and Jim Croxson, he soon had a roaring fire blazing in the big chapel stove. Two men, harnessing up Captain Murray's Dobbin with all possible haste, drove to the Branch for doctor and surgeon, for both were needed. Two

others, borrowing the largest waggon the town afforded, went off for a load of cots. There was something for every one to do, and every one was happy in doing it.

Meanwhile Captain Murray was hard at work in an effort to board the brig, with such of his crew as were still able to assist him. Three of his men had been helped or carried to their homes, too much exhausted and bruised to be of further service. When at last the little party had succeeded in reaching the brig, they had the good fortune to find the captain still alive, but unconscious from the ugly wound he had himself inflicted. They wasted no time in lowering the poor fellow into the surf-boat, and then made for the shore, for the vessel was fast going to pieces. The rescue of the Spanish captain completed the heroic labours of Epher Murray's crew for that morning, and the brave and wearied fellows went to their homes for a well-earned rest. Half-a-dozen fishermen volunteered their services to get the tackle once again in order. Indeed, none of the Moorlow people thought of setting about their regular occupations that eventful November morning, and all seemed proud to lend a hand in whatever way they could. Fortunately in a few hours the crew of the *Starling* were so far refreshed and rested as to be sent by the afternoon train to New York, where most of them lived when on land. There was literally no place in Moorlow where they could have been accommodated, unless in the chapel, that was fast being converted into a hospital. Sister Julia was superintending the work there, and by four o'clock everything was in readiness. Mrs. Murray had devoted her time to caring for the crew of the brig in the Life-saving Station. As soon as damp clothing had been removed, those who had sustained the severest injuries were made comfortable on mattresses brought from the bunks in the loft, and laid on the floor of the large room. The surgeon and doctor found considerable to do when they arrived, and the captain's wound claimed their first attention.

Sister Julia had remained to wait upon them, until all the bruises and wounds had been dressed. Meanwhile, Mrs. Murray had improved the opportunity to slip home and prepare a second breakfast, and Harry and Rex and Nan again trudged to and fro, laden with good things, only with much less difficulty now, for the storm had greatly abated.

All through that busy day of preparation, Ned and Hereward had kept up an incessant racing in and out of the chapel. Now and then they would brush against Sister Julia's black dress, and she could never resist the temptation, no matter how busy she might be, of giving them a friendly little pat. Then the two fellows would go bounding out of doors, as though through her touch they had received some special command which they must hasten to execute.

Early in the morning, to meet the first need of the surgeon, Sister Julia had taught some of the women, who were helping in the chapel, how to prepare a bandage. She showed them how they must tear off the muslin in strips, twice the width needed, and then must fold them evenly lengthwise through the centre, and cut them apart with scissors, because tearing both edges was likely to stretch them. Then she instructed them in the art of "rolling firmly," for there is not a more useless thing in the world than a poorly-rolled bandage. As she sat now by the side of one, and now by another, she would ask some simple question betraying her deep interest in them, and so more than one Moorlow woman, almost unconsciously, unburdened her heart to this new sweet friend, or told the story of her life. As Mr. Vale's work threw him into the company of many of the men, one after the other, he would enter into a friendly conversation with them, and some of the Moorlow men had their eyes opened to the fact that a minister might be something more than a mere preacher, standing quite apart from the common interests of their lives; that he might be an earnest, sympathetic man, a man subject to the same temptations and same trials as themselves, but able to rise above them, and even triumph in them, through the Spirit of God, which not only was in him, but which shone out in well-nigh every look and word and deed.

Oh! how welcome was the sight of the beds and the cheery fire to the eyes of those Spanish sailors, when they were tenderly carried into the chapel at sunset. Only a few hours before they had thought the bottom of the ocean would be the only bed they should ever know. No wonder their faces looked grateful and happy, notwithstanding every one of them was suffering more or less from the injuries he had received. When at last there was nothing more to be done, and with the exception of Sister Julia and her assistants the Moorlow folk were making ready to go home, the Spanish captain, who had regained consciousness soon after being brought ashore, beckoned to Mr. Vale. The poor fellow was quite too weak to speak, but knowing him to be a minister, he glanced round the chapel, and then, slightly raising his hand, pointed upward. Mr. Vale readily understood that the captain did not want the little company to break up till they had united in thanking God for the preservation of the crew of his vessel. Stepping into the reading desk, he easily gained the attention of everyone.

"The captain of the *Christina*," he said, "has indicated to me that he would like us to give God thanks for the rescue of

The Chapel

his crew. Will as many of you as are willing remain for a few moments?"

The women and children took their seats in the pews near which they were standing, and not a man went out. Never was a sweeter or more earnest service held in the little chapel, and there were tears in many eyes at its close. Every face looked tranquil and happy. For one whole day those Moorlow folk had not had so much as a thought of self, and nothing brings a happier look into the face than pure unselfishness. It had been a wonderful day for them all, and who of the number would ever forget it?

HIS LITTLE ROYAL HIGHNESS.

Out into the glow of the sunset and homeward went the little congregation, leaving Sister Julia and three or four women whom she had chosen as assistants in charge of the hospital. Regie and Harry and Nan, reluctant to leave, lingered in the doorway, till Sister Julia came and urged their going.

"Come, children," she said, "hurry home. Little Nan there looks ready to drop."

"Yes, I am tired," Nan admitted; "it has been such a long, long day," and without further urging the little trio trudged silently home; silently, because they had so much to think over. Two shipwrecks in one day! Regie remembered self-reproachfully that he had had his wish. For Nan, the excitement and fatigue had proved too much, and she fell asleep at the table before she had eaten a mouthful of supper, and knew nothing more till she woke late the next morning, with the sunlight streaming so brightly into her room as to make storms and shipwrecks seem the most improbable things that could ever happen.

XIV.

A Puzzling Question.

ITH so many willing hearts and hands at their service, it had been an easy matter to convert the chapel into a hospital; but now that it was converted, where was the money to come from to run it? The surgeon had said he thought it would be fully two weeks before the captain, and the two men who had been most badly hurt, would be about again, and in the meantime there were medicines to be bought and food to be provided for the entire party. Sister Julia knew well enough that there was no money to spare for the purpose in Moorlow, and they could hope for no remuneration from the poor sailors. With the wreck of his vessel and his cargo the captain himself had lost everything, and he had told Sister Julia "he had not even a penny left to go toward paying off his crew."

So it happened one afternoon, a day or two after the wreck, that Sister Julia, wrapping a shawl about her, left her patients in charge of her assistants, and went out on the beach to get a breath of fresh air, and try and think her way out of this money difficulty.

She had not gone far before she heard voices behind her, and turned to see Mr. Vale, with Regie and Harry and Nan, hurrying after her. They had hold of hands, and, stretched in one long line, looked like quite a formidable little party, as they came toward her.

"We have come to take you prisoner for neglect of duty," said Mr. Vale, as the line formed into a circle and shut her in.

"Not exactly neglect of duty," laughed Sister Julia; "my thoughts are all with the hospital. I have been racking my poor

brain to know where the money is to come from to support our patients up yonder."

"Yes, I knew that must be troubling you," Mr. Vale answered; "and I came down purposely to talk matters over with you. This log looks long enough to hold five people comfortably. Suppose we sit down here a few moments."

So they ranged themselves on the piece of timber, which had been stranded from the wreck of the *Starling*, and which two days of sunshine had thoroughly dried.

"Now," said Mr. Vale, "let us proceed to business. Suppose we have these men on our hands for two weeks, how much do you think it is going to cost us?"

"That is what I have been trying to get at," replied Sister Julia; "all the bedding and things must be paid for, and there is the coal, which we are burning at a lively rate the whole twenty-four hours. These women who help me can't afford to work without wages, though they would be willing enough to, and Bromley the sexton must have something, for he's up a dozen times a night tending to the fires in the two stoves. It seems to me ten dollars a day might be made to cover our running expenses, but I do not see how we can manage to do with less."

"That will be seventy dollars a week," said Harry, having worked out the difficult sum on the firm wet sand at his feet; "whew! but that's a lot, and for two weeks it would be twice that."

"Yes, a hundred and forty dollars," said Sister Julia; "it is a pretty large sum."

"And your own services ought not to go unremunerated," Mr. Vale suggested.

"Indeed they ought! I only wish my pocket were long enough to pay all the bills myself."

"I've wished mine was, a hundred times over, since the wreck."

"There's one thing I want to ask you, Mr. Vale," said Sister Julia, "and that is, if, after all, you think even my time is my own to give. You see while Mr. and Mrs. Fairfax are abroad I am employed by them to care for Reginald. To be sure he is so nearly well now that he does not need me, and Mrs. Murray is like a mother to him, but his lessons will have to be interrupted, and I wondered if Mr. Fairfax would feel I was doing quite right to neglect them."

"And who would care for the poor men then?" cried Nan, with real distress. "Nobody knows just how to do for 'em but you, Sister Julia."

"You need have no fears on the score of Mr. and Mrs.

Fairfax," said Mr. Vale, decidedly; "I know them well enough to assure you that they will thoroughly approve of and admire your course, and Nan is quite right. You know that no one here could care for them properly but just yourself."

"But how about the money?" urged Regie, who was anxious to know what they were going to do about it.

"Well, I have thought of two or three schemes," Mr. Vale replied. "You know we could write to Washington, and doubtless get an appropriation from some fund or other, but I would take a sort of pride in not bothering the Government at all about it; at any rate, not until we find it impossible to raise the sum ourselves."

"Say! Mr. Vale," said Rex, familiarly, "I'll tell you the very thing—take up a collection in your church next Sunday."

"Well, I hadn't thought of that, Rex," laughed Mr. Vale; "but, do you know, some of the good people there grumble already, thinking we have too many collections as it is. No, it seems to me it would be best to raise the money here if we could."

"But you can't," said Harry, emphatically, "there isn't any money here. I guess father has more than anyone in Moorlow, and yet I know he couldn't give much."

"Your father, Harry, has given his share, in the work he has done," Mr. Vale answered. "What I have to propose is this: suppose you and Reginald and Nan start out, say two days before Thanksgiving—that will be a week from next Tuesday—and take the village cart and Pet, and drive over to the Rumson Road. You know there are some well-to-do people living over there, who do not go back to town much before Christmas. Now they have every one heard by this time of the wreck of the *Christina*, and of the injuries her crew sustained, and I believe that every one of them would be glad to contribute, if you three little folks were to call upon them and tell them you were trying to raise two hundred dollars, which, you see, would cover all expenses. You know, at Thanksgiving time, people who have a great deal to be thankful for themselves often feel like helping other people who have not fared so well. It seems to me the plan is worth trying."

The children's faces plainly showed their delight in it.

"But how will we know where to go?" asked Nan.

"I will give you a list of half-a-dozen names," Mr. Vale replied. "I happen to have a little blank book in my pocket that is just what you need;" and, opening it, he wrote upon the first page, "Collection in Aid of the Crew of the *Christina*, wrecked off the Moorlow coast, November 12th, 18——."

Then underneath he wrote the words, "A Friend, $20."

"What do you mean by that?" asked Regie.

"I mean that I will give you twenty dollars to start the fund. Then, after you have been to all the other places, you must not forget to call upon my sister up at Mr. Avery's. She will be glad to give you something, I know, and Mr. Avery will, too, for that matter."

"I wish we could do it to-morrow," said Nan, whose enthusiasm always found it hard to brook delays of any sort.

"Oh, no, indeed!" Mr. Vale exclaimed, "you will get twice the money by waiting. Thanksgiving and Christmas have a magical way of letting down the bars to people's hearts, and making them more generous."

Of course Sister Julia entered into this fine plan as heartily as the children, and after they had talked a long while about it she bade them good-bye, and went back to her duties in the hospital a much cheerier woman than she had left it. The week that followed proved a long but happy one to the children. Long, because they were continually counting the days and the hours till the time should come when they could set out on that wonderful collecting tour; happy, in the unexpected holidays, which came to them through Sister Julia's inability to keep up their lessons. Surely every little scholar knows the peculiar charm of unlooked-for holidays.

By the common consent of the body-guard, the collecting-book had been placed in the keeping of his little Royal Highness, who had placed it for safety in the top drawer of his bureau. On the evening before they were to start on this momentous expedition, Regie had taken it out, handled it for several moments thoughtfully, and then put it back in its place, with an abstracted air, as though he was thinking very hard about something. Late that night, when the house was quiet, and every one asleep, he had crept noiselessly from bed, leaned out of the window to strike a match, for fear of waking Sister Julia in the next room, and lit his candle. Then, trying to keep a look out on all sides at once, as guiltily as any little thief, he went to the drawer, took out the little book, crossed to the table where the candle was standing, put a new pen in the holder, and then, with all the customary twists and twirls of his funny little mouth, wrote on a line, directly underneath Mr. Vale's,

"A Friend . . . . . . $20."

Then he sat, gazing proudly at it for fully five minutes before he put out the light and crept back to bed.

XV.

The Question Answered.

T was a bracing morning. Of course it was a November morning, for to-morrow would be Thanksgiving, and Mr. Vale stood looking out of his study window. It was a beautiful window in the spring and summer time, when the afternoon sun came streaming in through the Virginia creeper trained across it. Mr. Vale, who had the happiest way of looking at things, thought it a beautiful window, even in November. It might have opened on a blank wall, or a dull row of houses, as so many city windows do. Instead of that, it overlooked an old-fashioned garden, with little box-bordered flower-beds of every conceivable shape, and narrow gravel paths running between them. In some of the sunniest beds a few hardy chrysanthemums were still blooming, in brilliant reds and yellows. A fine western breeze was whistling through the leafless branches of the vine, and Mr. Vale drew in a long breath of the invigorating air. No doubt he would have drawn a still longer breath of the salt air he revelled in if he had been where his thoughts were, for they were down by the sea, where

at this very moment a little party was crowding into a village cart, about to start out on a long-talked-of expedition. If he could have looked into their earnest, rosy faces, and into their eyes brimming over with delight and expectation, I think he would have felt assured of the success of their undertaking. How could anyone resist such a winning troop of little beggars?

At last he closed the window, went back to his study table, and wrote out his Thanksgiving sermon, which he had been turning

over in his mind for many a day,—a glorious, invigorating sermon, as any member of the large congregation who heard it next day would have told you; but they could not have told you that it had won much of its inspiration from a little maiden who a few days before had looked up to him and said, with loving admiration, "I like your preaching; I like it very much indeed."

Well, the children were off at last, and they bowled along the hard boulevard road in the highest spirits. They crossed the Sea Bright Bridge, and Pet, who had not been over it since that

September morning when they went for the peaches, started to take the road that led to Burchard's orchard.

"No, sir-ree!" cried Regie, jerking him back, "we won't go there any more," and then the children laughed heartily over that eventful day's adventures, when the little red skirt had done such good service. Before long they found themselves in front of Mr. Allan's place, and his name came first on the list. It had been agreed between them that Regie should be spokesman for the party.

"You see, Harry," Nan had said, when they were discussing the matter in Regie's absence, "Regie has a kind of city way with him that is more taking, you know."

"I don't know anything of the kind," Harry had answered. "You're just gone over Regie. It's a pity you could not have had him for a brother instead of me."

"Now, Harry Murray," Nan replied, earnestly, "you know I would not exchange you for any brother in the world," which was pretty good of Nan, considering how large a share of teasing she had to undergo from this same Harry. The discussion had occurred several days previous to the expedition, and now that they had actually set out Harry was only too thankful that he did not have to play the principal part on the programme.

They drove up to the big house and tied Pet to a tree. No one was to be seen, and for a moment their hearts misgave them but it was too late to retrace their steps, and, with the air of a major domo, Harry marched proudly on to the piazza and pulled the bell, which was the special duty allotted to him. A coloured man in unpretentious livery opened the door.

"Does Mr. Allan live here?" asked Rex.

He hoped that the man did not notice that his voice trembled a little.

"Yes; would you like to see him?"

Before Rex could answer, "Yes, if you please," someone called from the back part of the house, "Is it three little children, Jackson?"

"Yes, sah, it is"

"Show them right in here, then," called the voice, and closing the door after them Jackson ushered them into a spacious dining-room, where an old gentleman sat toasting his feet and reading his morning paper before a crackling wood fire.

"Well, my little friends, I'm right glad to see you," he said, cordially. "You'll excuse my not getting up to meet you, I am such an old fellow, you know. Here, Jackson, put that little rocking-chair here near the fire for the young lady."

Nan looked about the room to see who the young lady might be.

"Oh! if you mean me," she said, laughing, taking her seat on a sofa, "I'm too warm to go near the fire, thank you."

"Pray be seated, gentlemen, and tell me what I can do for you," said Mr. Allan, turning to the boys.

"I guess you knew we were coming," Regie answered, sitting down in the nearest chair.

"What makes you think that?"

"Because you called to your man there as we came in to ask if it was not three little children, as though you were sort of expecting us."

"Oh, to be sure! but couldn't I have seen you as you drove up!"

"Not if you were sitting where you are now, sir," said honest Harry.

"Well, I guess I shall have to own up, then, that I did know you were coming. This is how I received my information," and Mr. Allan drew a little case from his pocket and began looking through the papers it contained. Nan gazed at the case in silent admiration. It was made of alligator skin, and had Mr. Allan's initials, R. T. A., in silver letters on the back.

"I wonder," she thought, "if two dollars would buy one like that for Regie when he goes home at Christmas time?"

And then she remembered with satisfaction that Regie had only two initials, which would probably make it come a little cheaper. Mr. Allan finally found a postal card, and handed it to Regie, who read aloud:—

"'NEW YORK, *November* 21*st*, 18—.

"'DEAR MR. ALLAN,—Three little friends of mine will call on you to-morrow. I hope they will be none the less welcome when they have told you their errand.

"'Yours in haste,

"'F. F. VALE.'"

"Then you do not know what we have come for," and Regie produced his collecting book with a most business like air. Mr. Allan put on his spectacles and examined it carefully. "Oh, I see," he said at last, "you are collecting for the poor sailors who were saved from the wreck. I hear you turned the church into a hospital. You could not have done a better thing."

"Yes, we did," said Nan, proudly, "and the sailors are all very nice men indeed, and if it had not been for Sister Julia's care, two of them would have died."

"And who is Sister Julia?"

"Don't you know who Sister Julia is?" she asked, incredulously; "why, I thought everyone in New York knew about her. She's——"

"Let Regie tell," Harry interrupted. "You see he has a kind of city way with him that is more taking, you know," he added, with a sly wink and in tones too low for Mr. Allan's ear.

Nan immediately relapsed into silence, and Regie came to the front.

"Sister Julia is a nurse, but she's a lady too, and she came to Moorlow to take care of me when I broke my leg last June. She lives in a great hospital in New York, and takes care of sick people, mostly children."

"But how does she happen to be here now?" asked Mr. Allan. "Those two legs of yours seem to be as strong as anybody's."

"Oh, yes, it's all right now," and Regie regarded his right leg rather affectionately; "but Sister Julia stayed on to look after me, because Papa and Mamma Fairfax have gone to Europe."

"Then you are Curtis Fairfax's adopted boy?" Mr. Allan exclaimed with some surprise; and readjusting his gold-rimmed spectacles he looked Regie over rather critically.

"Yes, sir, I am," Rex replied, for almost the first time in his life hearing that word "adopted" without wincing.

"You'll do well then if you make as good a man as your father. He's one of the whitest men in the trade."

Regie did not quite know what he meant by that, but hesitated to ask.

"Just how are you going to use this money?" asked Mr. Allan.

"For the hospital, sir. It costs seventy dollars a week to run it. The brig was wrecked last week, Wednesday you know, and Sister Julia says they will not be able to go before the middle of next week, so we need a hundred and forty dollars, and sixty dollars more for beds and other things."

Mr. Allan re-opened the little book.

"I see," he said, "that you have forty dollars promised already. I recognise Mr. Vale's hand in this first twenty. Are you free to tell who contributes the other?"

"The other twenty!" exclaimed Harry, looking over Mr. Allan's shoulder; "why, that is Regie's writing!"

Rex coloured up to the roots of his brown hair, as though he had been the most guilty of little culprits.

"I have ten dollars now of my own," he stammered, "and I know of a way I can surely earn ten more when I get back to town, so I am going to ask Mr. Vale to lend me the money."

"Good for you!" said Mr. Allan, "I call that downright generous, and as I happen to know of a way I can earn sixty dollars when I get back to town, I suppose I ought to put myself down for forty at any rate. I guess I had better draw a check to your order, as you seem to be chairman of the committee," and crossing the room he sat down at a little oak desk. Nan stared at Rex in mute amazement. She had never dreamed he was such a wealthy personage. Harry's respect was wonderfully increased too, by the way. To think that a boy no older than he actually knew of a way by which he could earn ten dollars! He stowed that piece of information away in his mind as a matter to be inquired into more particularly at a later date, and was so ungracious as to have some doubts as to the perfect truthfulness of the statement. Just at this moment Jackson came again into the room, bearing a tray laden with cider and doughnuts; clear, amber-coloured cider, in a cut-glass pitcher, and doughnuts generously sprinkled with powdered sugar, and fried that morning.

"I thought dese yere children might enjoy a little sumfin' to eat arter their long ride this breezy morning," said Jackson, setting the tray on the table.

"A happy thought, Jackson," answered Mr. Allan, smiling; "and now suppose we draw up to the table and be comfortable."

The children needed no urging, and Jackson, placing a plate in front of each of them, passed the doughnuts, and then filled four tempting little tumblers to the brim.

"Let us drink to the health of Sister Julia," said Mr. Allan, and he was greatly amused at the easy grace with which the children complied.

Captain Murray had once taken Nan and Harry to a "Rip Van Winkle" *matinée*, and so they chanced to know what was the proper thing to do when a health was proposed. Afterward, Harry proposed the health of Mr. Vale, because, as he put it, "he was such a brick at the time of the wreck;" and then Regie proposed Captain Murray's. Altogether it was a very merry party, and the children finally bade Mr. Allan a reluctant good-bye, when Rex decided that "they really ought to go on to the next place, for if they kept on at this rate they wouldn't get home till morning."

They had still four names on their list, and already had half the money.

Feeling sure that Mr. Vale had in each place heralded their coming by a postal, they entered the other houses with an air of childish confidence which seemed to say, "We have called for that money, please."

Everywhere they were received with more than cordial kindness, and when Pet turned his head homeward the whole amount had been subscribed.

"Oh, dear me!" Nan suddenly exclaimed, quite overcome by a thought that had occurred to her.

"What is it, goosie?" And it is not necessary to mention who asked that.

"Why, we have all the money we need, and we have not called on Miss Vale yet."

"That's so, by cracky!" said Harry.

"Well, we'll just have to go there and explain," Rex volunteered.

"Perhaps you had better not give so much yourself," suggested Harry; "I don't see how you are ever going to earn ten dollars."

"Well, I do then," in a kingly way, resenting such interference."

"Oh yes, we ought to go," said Nan; "I only hope she won't mind our having collected it all."

It did not occur to either of this committee (and would there were more of these sort of people in the world!) that anyone might possibly prefer not being called upon for a subscription. They themselves regarded the opportunity for giving in the light of an actual privilege. Nan was thankful the money was so easily raised, for she had not a penny in the world to give save that two dollars, which she must reserve for that little wallet for Regie; but she was planning to present a warm comforter, which her own little hands had made, to the Spanish captain, and she thought she might favour the first mate with the rubber pencil-case which she had bought as a parting present for Regie.

When they reached Mr. Avery's they found Miss Vale ready to receive them. She was very much of an invalid, seldom able to leave her room, but in honour of their coming she had put on a pretty wrapper, and was seated in a large rocking-chair. She was anxious to meet these little friends of whom her brother had so often spoken, and looked forward to their coming as quite an event in her quiet life. The nurse led the children up the oaken stair, and Nan trod as noiselessly as possible herself, but was sure she had never heard Harry and Regie make such a noise before.

Miss Vale received them very cordially, and they felt at home with her at once. They talked about the wreck for some time, and then Miss Vale said, "Well, I believe you want some money from me for the hospital?"

"No," Nan answered, with much seriousness, and as though she was breaking the saddest piece of news imaginable; "we are very sorry, but we don't need any more; we got enough money before we knew it. We couldn't help it, really."

Nan saw that the nurse was laughing in a quiet way, but never dreamt that she was the cause of the merriment. Miss Vale herself looked amused, but managed to keep her face straight as she said, feigning much anxiety, "Dear me! what am I to do, then? I had made up my mind to give you a hundred dollars."

The finance committee looked puzzled enough, and as though they saw no way out of this difficulty.

"But look here," Miss Vale continued, "I have an idea. The captain and his crew did not save anything from the wreck, did they?"

"Not a thing, and some of them haven't a penny in the world," Harry answered.

"How many are there?"

"Seven," answered the children, in one breath.

"Well then, wouldn't it be a good thing to divide the money among them, so that they will have something to begin life with again?"

"Seven won't go into a hundred evenly," said Harry, having a horror of fractions.

"Well, I guess we can fix matters if it doesn't," was Regie's scornful response. "I think it is very kind of you," turning to Miss Vale. "When shall we give it to them?"

"It seems to me to-morrow would be a good day. Are the men to have a Thanksgiving dinner?"

"Indeed they are," Nan answered. "They are to have turkey, and mashed potatoes, and cranberries that mother has made in beautiful moulds, and mince-pie, and lots of things. They'll all be able to come to the table too, except the captain."

"It's just as well that he can't come," Regie explained, with the air of an experienced doctor. "He isn't strong enough to eat turkey dna hearty things like that."

"He's to have some very nice gruel, though," Nan confided, and as though she knew more about it all than both the boys put together; as indeed she did, for she had been present at many a conference between Sister Julia and her mother regarding the dinner.

The children made a long call, and no one knows how much longer they would have lingered in Miss Vale's sunny room, looking at some fine photographs of Mr. Avery's, which the maid had brought up from the parlour, if the old clock in the hall had not struck two very clearly and distinctly.

"Is it as late as that?" cried Nan; "we shall miss our dinner altogether if we don't go home this minute."

That was sufficient to start the boys, and the children took their departure, Miss Vale promising to send the money down that night in separate envelopes, so that Harry should not be bothered by the difficult division of one hundred by seven.

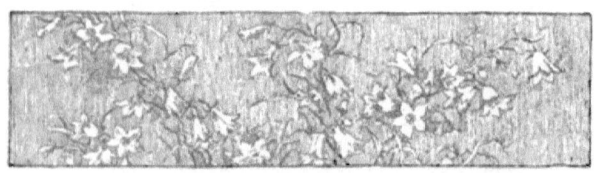

XVI.

The Captain's Story.

T is only quite natural that the little folks throughout these United States should set less store by Thanksgiving day than Christmas. It may seem all very fine to sit down to a Thanksgiving dinner, but, after all, Thanksgiving may not hold a candle to Christmas,—to Christmas, with its continued round of excitement, beginning in the small hours of the morning with the inspection of Christmas presents, and ending, in all probability, with the glory and glitter of a well-loaded Christmas tree at night. Yet I doubt if the most favoured little darling in the world, who knew every wish for a twelvemonth would find its fulfilment on Christmas morning, ever looked forward to that day as eagerly as our little friends to this Thanksgiving.

I will do them the credit to say that they gave little thought to the good things that were to fall to their own share. They were each conjuring pictures for themselves of how those Spanish sailors would look when they sat down to that good dinner. Two of the sailors knew nothing of English beyond the two words "thank you." Nan could see them now saying it with their funny accent every time anything was passed to them. And when she wondered how they would look when the money was handed to them, she could hardly wait for the glad moment to come and see for herself. She did not have to wait long, for those were her last thoughts before falling asleep, and when she awoke it was Thanksgiving morning. Of course the weather would have much to do with the pleasure of the day, so the first thing she did was to fly to the window and throw open the blinds. The late November sun, rising out of the ocean, flooded everything with a rosy light, and the air was mild enough for early

October. Three or four seagulls were sailing over the waves in search of their breakfast, making a dive now and then when their wonderful far-reaching gaze detected a fish near the surface of the water. Nan watched one of them circling round and round, and clapped her hands from sheer delight when she saw him rise from a desperate dive with a fish quivering in his talons, then flying homeward to his nest on the bough of some inland tree. It seemed as though even the seagulls ought to fare better than on other days. To be sure it put a sad ending to the life of the poor little fish, but no doubt it was as allowable for seagulls to dine off men-haden, as for people to dine off roast turkeys and ducks. This logical train of thought, and some other thoughts not as logical, tripped through Nan's mind as she made her neat little toilet. The brown hair was braided quickly but very evenly, and tied with a scarlet ribbon; the whitest of little yoke-aprons was put on over the blue flannel dress, and, notwithstanding it opened down the back and boasted fifteen buttons, was carefully adjusted by Nan's own little fingers. It is astonishing what "own little fingers" can do for the children who must needs wait on themselves.

A radiant embodiment of sweetness and freshness, Nan bustled into the dining-room, to find the boys there before her. They were curled up on the window-seat looking over, for perhaps the tenth time, the budget of envelopes which Miss Vale had sent the night before.

"You look good enough to eat this morning," said Harry, with a look of honest admiration.

"Well, I guess I shall not be good enough to let you eat me," Nan answered, blushing a little.

Harry caught her dress as she passed him, and held her firmly while he gave her the heartiest sort of a kiss. The truth is that two months ago Harry would have done nothing of the sort. It might have occurred to him, but he simply would not have done it. Regie had been teaching him a lesson. Always gallant and thoughtful himself toward Nan, Harry had watched him closely, and gradually had come to the conclusion that a brother might really treat his sister with much consideration without being set down for a spoony; indeed, might even go so far as to actually express his admiration, not only in words, but in the deed of an unexpected kiss now and then, without being silly. The lesson was well worth learning, and would it might be taught to a host of well-meaning little Harrys, who need to learn it every whit as much as this Harry in particular! As soon as Sister Julia arrived they had breakfast. She ran up every morning from the hospital, for the sake of the change and fresh air. As soon as the meal was finished, preparations were at once begun for the great Thanksgiving dinner. In the first place Dobbin was brought to the door, and the two boys helped Captain Murray carry out from the hall several well-filled boxes and baskets; for the dinner was to be served in the rear end of the chapel, as Captain Murray's dining-room was too small to accommodate so large a party comfortably; besides, one or two of the men were not so far recovered as to be able to venture out of doors. Pet and the cart were also pressed into service, and made numerous trips to and fro, until at last, with the help of the sailors, everything had been unloaded at the chapel door.

Mrs. Murray, in a long white apron, presided over the cooking, and soon a strange new incense, which was none other than the smell of roasting turkey, began to make its way to the rafters of the church.

The captain on his cot sniffed it gratefully, and he wished from the bottom of his heart that he was up and about and able to enjoy it. Sister Julia busied herself with setting the table. Rex and Harry sat in one corner paring potatoes, and the sailors strolled about with their hands in their pockets, and broad smiles on their dark faces, rendering some little service whenever they could.

The one who could not speak English at all kept near Mrs. Murray, watching her intently with his large black eyes, and trying to anticipate any little thing he might do for her, such as lifting the great pot, in which a savoury soup was boiling away, or pushing more wood into the cooking-stove.

"Well, Sister Julia, what can I do now?" asked Nan, when she had finished the glasses.

"Let me see," answered Sister Julia, pausing a second to count the places at the table, to be sure she had made no mistake; "I think you might arrange the fruit. The bananas and oranges will look the better for a careful rubbing with one of the glass towels."

"All right," Nan said, cheerily, glad to have so important a task assigned to her. Just as she had gotten everything together a sudden thought occurred to her, and seizing a fruit dish under each arm, she travelled down the aisles and into the vestry.

During the week she and the Spanish captain had grown to be fast friends, and his face brightened the moment he saw her.

"I was thinking you might be a little lonely," she said; "if you like, I can bring my work in here and do it."

"Indeed, senorita, nothing would please me better," the captain answered, in musical broken English. The captain always addressed Nan as "senorita," the pretty word that stands for miss in his native tongue.

Nan asked two of the sailors to carry the great box of oranges and bananas into the vestry, and seating herself on the floor, with a dish on each side of her, she set to work.

"How do you feel to-day, captain?" she asked, by way of opening the conversation, and rubbing vigorously away at an orange.

"Better, senorita; but one does not want to get well too fast, and say good-bye to Sister Julia and the rest of you who have been so kind to us all."

"You are sorry, then, that you tried to do it, aren't you?"

"Do what, senorita?" and the colour came into his dark face.

"Why, kill yourself, captain," polishing away at a banana without looking up, and feeling pretty sure it would have been better not to have said this.

"I had hoped the little senorita did not know about that," sighed the captain. "It was a cowardly and foolish thing to do."

"It was a very wicked thing, captain. I hope you never will try to do it again."

"Never you fear," he answered, smiling; "all my life I will try to make amends for it; and I will tell you something you may think strange, senorita, and that is, that this has been the happiest week in all my life. Two or three times when I have been lying here, just at sunset, where I could watch the great white breakers come rolling in, and Sister Julia has been playing on the organ in the church there, I have thought I must be dreaming in my berth in the poor *Christina*. Then I have raised myself on my elbow, so that I could look into the chancel yonder and see the cross on the altar cloth, and feel sure it was really all as it seemed."

"You are not exactly glad you were wrecked, though?" Nan asked, practically.

"Yes, in a way, I am glad."

"You don't forget about losing all your money and things, do you?"

"No, but perhaps it's worth while to have lost one's money to be wrecked on a coast of big and little angels."

"Big and little angels!"

"Yes, and if you want to know why it seems so to me you must listen to a story."

There was no "must listen" for Nan where a story was concerned. She was all attention in a moment, an eager breathless little listener, and the captain began.

"Just thirty-six years ago a Spanish boy found himself without father or mother, and was set adrift on the world. Not a penny did he own, but he was a hearty, fearless little fellow, and he managed somehow to live, though he seldom knew where the next meal was to come from, or where he would sleep at night. By the time the boy was ten years old he grew tired of his vagabond life, and longed to learn how to read and write. So he resolved to go to the village school, and he earned a little money out of school hours here and there, and was a happier fellow than in the old idle days.

"No sooner had he learned to read and write in pretty decent fashion than he decided to run away to sea, for he had always a notion that he would be a sailor some day. I do not know that you could exactly call it running away, when no one cared very much whether he came or went; but for the next few years he had a pretty hard time of it, for to go to sea before the mast under a harsh and cruel captain is likely to make life rather difficult. Sometimes when he was sent out to reef the top-gallant sail he would balance himself on the yard, wondering if it would not be better to let himself drop into the ocean—the men would only think he had tumbled off; but somehow the fear of God always kept him from it.

"Notwithstanding the hardship he went to sea again until he

was twenty-five years old, and by that time he had worked up to be first mate of the——"

"Of the *Christina?*" Nan questioned, eagerly.

"Yes, of the *Christina*," the captain admitted; "and he had managed to save enough to become part owner of her besides."

Nan had finished her work, but was quite unmindful of the

fact, and sat gazing up to the captain's face, with her hands clasped round her knees.

"Had he grown up to be a good man?" she asked, innocently.

"I am afraid not, senorita, as you would count goodness."

"Was he kind to his men?" altogether unconscious of how embarrassing her questions might prove.

"Yes, he was kind. That was the best thing that could be said for him. He did not deserve any credit for that, though, for he had suffered so much himself from unkindness."

"Then he deserved all the more credit," Nan said, decidedly, and the colour in the captain's face showed how grateful her praise was to him.

"Well, it happened one November morning," he continued, "ten years afterward, that when he had been battling all night with the wind and the waves of a terrible storm, his ship ran ashore, and in such a way that he knew he could never save her. All the earnings of his lifetime gone in a minute! What was there to live for? He had not a relative in the world, and that ship was his darling. Then the thought to take his own life came to him, as it used to sometimes when he was a poor little sailor on the top-gallant yard, only now that he was a man no thought of God came with it, and so the desperate deed was attempted."

Nan had never listened to anything so fascinating in all her life before.

"That is not all?" she asked, eagerly, for the captain had paused for a moment.

"Thank God, no! scarcely did the captain—for he was no longer first mate—think that the ugly weapon had done its work, than he seemed to be all by himself in a beautiful silver boat on a wide blue sea. It was a little boat, without sails or oars, and it bounded over the waves of its own free will, so that the captain had simply to let it carry him whither it would. Soon he knew they were nearing a shore, for he recognised the sound of breakers on the beach; but he shuddered as he heard it, for he half-remembered that something terrible had happened when he had heard that sound once before. But his fright was over in a moment, for he saw a great banner waving in the air, and on it was printed, in gold letters, 'The Shore of Lovingkindness.'

"As he neared the land, one curling white breaker seemed gently to lift the boat on to the next, until at last it was landed on a great white stretch of beach. It seemed to the captain such a beautiful shore, that he wondered if it might be heaven, and if it was, he knew he had no right there. He tried to lift himself up and step out of the little boat, but somehow he was not able to do that; so he lay quite still and contented, looking up at the stars overhead,—wonderful stars they were, for the only light there was came from them, and yet he could see everything plainly. At last the stars seemed to grow dim and still more dim, and the captain turned himself over on the silk cushions of the boat and fell asleep. When he awoke he stared about him with a wondering gaze, for everything looked so strange. He

was no longer in the silk-cushioned boat, but lying on a cot in a little room, a queer little room, with a carved oaken partition, and soft red curtains running along two sides of it. He could not see very plainly, for the light was low in the room, and he could not tell where it came from. He felt something heavy on his head, and put his hand up, for he remembered that he had thought that the little red boat had landed him in heaven. But alas! there was no crown, only a tightly-bound bandage, and the moment his hand touched it he guessed why it was there, and that he was only a shipwrecked captain whom someone had cared for. But where was he? A door led out of his little room—into what? Why, it looked like a church; yes, it was surely a church, for the moonlight was streaming through the chancel window, and he could see the communion table and some one sitting beyond the chancel rail. How strange! What could it mean? He put his hand to his head again to make sure of the bandage, and that he was not dreaming. And now the figure has left the table, and is moving toward him. It comes gently to the side of his cot, and he can see that it is a woman, a woman with the face of an angel. The captain looks up at her with a wondering gaze; but she puts her finger to her lips as a sign that he must not speak. Then she makes the light brighter in the room, and draws a chair to his side, and tells him in a low, sweet voice all about himself—how he happens to be in the vestry of the little church; and finally she tells him that she means to take care of him until he is entirely well again. But the captain almost wishes he may never be well again, if he may only have that angel face to watch over him."

"That angel was Sister Julia," said Nan, with a sigh, as though to relieve her overcharged little heart.

"Yes, that was Sister Julia," assented the captain.

"But you said there were little angels, too," Nan said, innocently.

"Certainly. I have a picture of the little *arch*angel (that is, the principal one) here beside me," and the captain placed a little frame in Nan's eager hands.

Of course it proved to be only a little mirror, in which she saw the reflection of her own fair little face.

"Do you call a round chubby face like that the face of an angel?" she laughed, holding the little mirror at arm's length and looking in, in a funny, half-critical fashion.

"Yes, I do. It has been a real angel face to me, coming in and out of this vestry room with its bright smiles."

"Why, where is Nan?" someone called just then.

"Coming, Sister Julia," Nan answered, jumping to her feet, and with an effort lifting one of the heavy fruit dishes.

"I must go," she said, reluctantly; but when she reached the door she paused for a moment to look back and ask, "It *was* true, wasn't it, all that about when you were a boy; all except about the boat and the angels?"

"Every word of it," answered the captain; "and it was true about the angels, too, senorita."

XVII.

Thanksgiving in Earnest.

THE hour-hand of the watch that hung at Sister Julia's belt had just reached three as she put the last touch to the table; that last touch consisted in placing, at each seat, a card bearing the name of the person who was to occupy it. Sister Julia had herself prepared the cards in the little leisure she could spare from hospital duties. On each she had painted some little emblem of the sea—a shell, or a spray of seaweed—introducing the name in odd-shaped letters.

Then on the reverse side she had enrolled the entire party in the order of their seats at the table, knowing that some of their number would cherish those little cards as precious souvenirs for many a long year to come.

The soup was on the table, and Mrs. Murray having instructed the woman who had been helping her just how to bring the dishes to the table, laid aside her great gingham apron, and gave the signal to sit down.

"Why, there's one seat too many!" remarked Harry, when all had found their places.

"Dear me, why so there is!" exclaimed Sister Julia. "How did that ever happen?"

"Why, it happened just this way," answered a familiar voice; no one could tell just where the voice came from, but all knew whose it was. "It happened just this way. I telegraphed Sister Julia yesterday that if she would put off the dinner till three o'clock I could get through my sermon in time to come, and so here I am, you see," and Mr. Vale appeared in the door-way, having waited a moment in the vestibule to hang up his coat.

The presence of Mr. Vale was just the one thing needed to complete that Thanksgiving dinner in everyone's estimation.

Even the men, whose knowledge of English was limited to the parrot-learned "Thank you," brightened when they saw him. There are faces which bear so plainly the imprint of love and sympathy, one does not need to speak a common language to comprehend them.

"You have come at the right moment," said Sister Julia, and Mr. Vale, knowing what she meant, bowed his head and asked a blessing. It was a prayer as well as a blessing—a prayer for the future of these sailors, who were so soon again to give their lives to the keeping of the sea; and a prayer for the future of the children, that the whole volume of their life might remain as pure and unsullied as the pages of their childhood—nor did he forget the captain lying on his cot in the little vestry room. His voice seemed to gather additional earnestness as he prayed that he might be restored to perfect health, and take up his life again with a divine trust and courage which should be able to grapple victoriously with misfortune and despair, should he again be called to meet them.

At the close of the blessing Sister Julia thought she heard a low fervent "Amen" from the recesses of the little vestry room.

No doubt it was but natural that everyone at that long table should realise that it was no ordinary occasion. Never did a stranger company sit down to a Thanksgiving dinner under stranger circumstances, but they enjoyed it heartily, notwithstanding the strangeness.

Somehow or other, Mr. Vale knew just the way to draw everybody out, and thanks to him the party, that otherwise might easily have found itself a little stiff and embarrassed, became a very merry one. Captain Murray enlivened the table with two or three old sea yarns, and while they were waiting for the dessert to be brought in Mr. Vale induced the sailors to give them two or three Spanish songs which they were accustomed to sing together at sea. Meanwhile, Nan had travelled into the vestry with the captain's dinner, of clam broth and dainty little crackers; delicious broth, which Sister Julia had herself prepared, and crackers which Nan's own little hands had toasted to a most inviting brownness. It did Nan's heart good to see how the captain enjoyed eating them, and it did the captain's heart good to see how much she enjoyed seeing him eat them; and so it was that all through that Thanksgiving Day a constant process of *doing hearts good* seemed to be going on, on every side.

When at last Mrs. Murray lifted an all-on-fire plum pudding to the table, one of the younger sailors, who was little more than a boy, clapped his hands from sheer delight, and, fired by his enthusiasm, all at the table followed his example. The colour came into Mrs. Murray's round face; she considered the demonstration as a compliment to herself, as was quite right she should, for no little raisin-stoning and washing of currants had gone toward the concoction of that great brown pudding, about which the blue flames were now curling so beautifully.

At last the supreme moment for "all hands" arrived, when, at a signal from Sister Julia, Regie, as chairman of the finance committee, produced the budget of envelopes, and handed them to one and another as fast as he could make out the names written on the backs of them.

Meanwhile, Mr. Vale stood up, and explained that each envelope contained a gift of money, and though by no means a large amount, the giver hoped it might stand them in good stead, and that each would kindly accept it with her best wishes.

At the words "her best wishes," the eyes of the crew, as by common consent, turned toward Sister Julia, so that she had right away to deny having had any part in the transaction.

"No, indeed," she said, "you must not thank me for this; Mr. Vale's sister is the good friend to whom you are indebted."

In the absence of their captain the men looked to their first mate to express their gratitude. Mr. Vale would have given a great deal if his sister could have heard the few earnest words which the first mate spoke from a full heart, and could have seen the sturdy fellow as he spoke them.

And so the dinner was ended. It had grown quite dark in the chapel, for the early November twilight had deepened landward and seaward.

"Before we separate," said Mr. Vale, "I wish Regie would sing the German evening hymn from the Children's Hymnal."

Regie needed no urging, and took his stand beside Sister Julia at the organ, while the others still kept their places. He loved to sing, throwing his whole soul into it, and in that lay half his power to please.

Clear and sweet rang out the words of the simple hymn, and at its close more than one sleeve was brushed across misty eyes, and tears stole from under the captain's eyelids as he lay in the little vestry—lying there alone, why need he strive to hide them?—besides, what was there to be ashamed of in such tears as those?

These had been days of new and strange experiences to those Spanish sailors, and they had learned some of life's best lessons for the first time.

"Your faces are kinder than when you came," Nan had frankly said to the crew one day.

"Senorita, that is because our hearts are kinder," one of the men had answered.

XVIII.

The King's Camera.

NOTHER week rolled by, and found the crew of the *Christina* ready to say good-bye to Moorlow, and yet not ready, for most of them were very loth to go; but the captain was quite recovered, and there was no excuse for their remaining longer. Indeed, Sister Julia thought that those of their number who had sustained no very severe injuries ought to have gone before, but the men seemed anxious to stand by their captain, and she did not quite have the courage to send them off. That such a sad state of things was possible never seemed to enter the mind of any member of the crew. Without being in any sense ungrateful, they simply took everything for granted. With the exception of the captain, not one of them ever questioned where the money came from that provided so generously for their wants during those two weeks. They looked upon Sister Julia as a veritable saint, with illimitable, if not divine, resources, sent to minister to them especially; and the reverential way in which they bade her farewell showed that they so regarded her to the last.

All Moorlow was gathered at the station to see them off. Everyone who had contributed in any way to their comfort,—and there were few in Moorlow who had not—felt a sort of responsibility in giving them a cheery "send off." Even the shabby little Croxsons were there, for had they not run on innumerable errands that morning when the crew were rescued? As the train moved away the captain stood upon the rear platform. A neat little bundle was tucked under one arm, for Nan, not forgetting her resolution, had presented him at the last moment with the warm comforter which she herself had made. The captain waved a red handkerchief until the station was entirely out of sight, and his last glance, before he turned and went into the car, was toward the hull of the *Christina*, which he could plainly see just where she had stranded that stormy November morning. It seemed to him as though he were saying good-bye to all his past, and with a courage that surprised him he was ready to make a new start. He was very grateful for the fact that his men were thoroughly loyal to him, and felt pretty sure that with such a crew at his service he could easily gain command of some vessel plying between Spain and the United States. So it was that with a contented smile he took a seat in the midst of his crew, and, encouraged by their captain's good cheer, the dark-eyed men soon fell to conversing in the liveliest manner in their native Spanish, much to the amusement of their fellow-passengers.

It had been a very exciting fortnight for quiet Moorlow, but in a marvellously short space of time everything settled back into the old grooves. The little church soon looked as sober and decorous as though it had never served as a temporary hospital, or known the savoury odours of a Thanksgiving dinner.

A December storm had beaten the *Christina's* hull literally to pieces, and nothing was left to tell the story of the wreck save the shell which had been shot out with the whip-line, and which Captain Murray, according to custom, had lettered and dated, and hung in the Life-saving Station; a trophy of which the crew had good reason to be proud.

The children had resumed their lessons, and Regie was counting the days till Papa and Mamma Fairfax would board the homeward-bound steamer at Liverpool. The three months, which had seemed a long time to look forward to, had slipped away very quickly, and Harry and Nan and himself were full of joyous anticipation, for a glorious plan was on foot.

Mr. Fairfax had written very urgently asking that the Murray children might be allowed to spend the Christmas holidays with Regie in town. Captain Murray had only given his consent very reluctantly, for he knew the Moorlow Christmas would be a sorry affair without the children; but nevertheless he *had* given it, and Nan and Harry's respective heads were almost turned with delight at the prospect.

It is doubtful if the liveliest imagination could picture all that a whole week in New York meant to these little Murrays. They had never been there for more than a day at a time, and then only at rare intervals, and it was not strange that stolen whispers in lesson hours, and long chats out of them, all bore upon the delightful subject of this visit, until, in Sister Julia's estimation, the children were devoting too much time to sitting indoors, and plotting and planning, and not enough to out-of-door exercise; so she put her wits to work to devise some scheme to bring about a change of affairs.

"There is one thing, Regie," she said, "over which your Papa Fairfax will be very much disappointed when he comes home."

She spoke so seriously, that Regie looked up at her with a very troubled face, which said as plainly as words, "Whatever do you mean?"

"Why, you haven't a single picture to show him. In all this while not a photograph have you taken."

"That's so," with a sigh; "but then I don't believe he'll expect it. You can't do much photographing in cold weather; besides, there's nothing to take in winter."

"You said once that you'd like to take a good picture of me," Nan remarked, showing that she did not consider that the low state of the thermometer in any way diminished her charms, as indeed it did not. There was not a prettier or more breezy little specimen of humanity in existence than Nan on one of these wintry afternoons, when she had just come in from an hour's buffeting with wind and weather on the beach.

"Yes, I *would* like a good picture of you, Nan," said Regie, patronisingly, looking at her with his head on one side, after the meditative fashion of an artist regarding his model. "The trouble is, I don't know of any place in this house where you can get a good enough light."

"And why in the house, pray?" asked Sister Julia; "it is not a bit too cold to try your hand out of doors. This is just a perfect winter's day, and there is no wind to blow your camera over."

"That's so," assented Regie again, "I'm going to get ready," and suiting the action to the word he bounded out of the room, and the body-guard followed his example.

At the time that Mr. Fairfax had seen fit to endow Regie with a photographing outfit, he had, with no little painstaking, carefully instructed him as just to how the whole process, from beginning to end, must be managed. As a result Regie had succeeded in producing some first-rate pictures, "all his own work, too," as he would have told you proudly. But that was more than a year ago, and before he knew Nan and Harry. He had some fine plans for the summer just ended, but that unlucky fall from the cherry tree bough had prevented his carrying them out. To be sure, within the last few weeks, since the little leg had so thoroughly mended, he might have gotten to work again as easily as could be, but the excitement following the wreck of the *Christina* had driven all thought of it out of his mind.

The fact that Nan knew that Regie could take pictures accounted in a measure, perhaps, for the reverence with which she regarded him; but Harry was as doubtful of his real ability as in the matter of the earning of the money for the hospital fund, and he hailed with delight the chance he was about to have to put him to the test.

Harry and Nan were ready in no time, but with the amateur photographer, "getting ready" is a mysterious and laborious proceeding, and Rex failed to put in an appearance.

The body-guard waited and waited till, their patience exhausted, they scaled the stairway leading to His Royal Highness's private apartment, but His Majesty was nowhere to be seen.

"Why, where is Rex?" cried Nan.

"I'm in here," answered a muffled voice.

"What, in the closet?" and Harry rushed for it.

"Yes, but don't open the door for the world. I'm filling my plate-holders."

Harry and Nan looked at each other as much as to say, "What in creation is he talking about?" then by tacit consent they noiselessly crouched down by the closet door, and Harry peeped through the keyhole.

His face grew pale, and with a terrified expression he drew Nan over so that she could take a look; then with precipitate haste they fled from the room.

"Oh, Sister Julia!" cried Nan.

"Regie's shut up in his closet," cried Harry.

"And we looked through the keyhole and saw an awful red light," interrupted Nan.

"And we think he has set the closet on fire, and you had better go and see to it right away," interrupted Harry, very much surprised that Sister Julia did not seem in the least alarmed.

"Why, he's only filling his plate-holders," she exclaimed, laughing.

"Yes," nodded Nan, her eyes as large as saucers, "he said something like that."

"Of course he did, and the fire you thought you saw is the light from his ruby lantern."

"His what!" exclaimed Harry; then, after a little pause, he added, "Say! won't you explain to us something about it?" Ashamed that he had shared Nan's fright, and foreseeing that he would be obliged to ask Regie more questions than would be at all agreeable.

"Why, certainly," answered Sister Julia, with a smile still playing about the corners of her mouth. "You see they take these pictures on a plate, that is a square glass which comes for the purpose, coated with a dry, white preparation. Mr. Fairfax buys them in boxes holding a dozen each, and when Regie wants to take pictures he has to take them from the box and put them in his plate-holders. The plate-holders are a sort of little boxes that fit in the back of his camera."

"His cam-e-ra?" drawled Nan.

"Yes, that is the name of the instrument he takes the pictures with, but it will ruin the plate to let a ray of daylight touch it

before he is ready to take the picture, so Rex must needs go into a dark closet, and light his ruby lantern, when the time comes for filling his plate-holders."

Regie appeared on the scene just then, with his apparatus in his arms, and the trio marched off, the King all unconscious of the fright he had given the body-guard, and the body-guard intending never to enlighten him on the subject.

"What shall we take?" said Regie, when they had gone a

little way down the beach. "I wish we had enough for a group. I like to take groups best."

"What is a group?" Nan asked, shyly.

"Why, a group's a lot of people, goosie," Harry answered, for he enjoyed answering questions in direct proportion to his dislike to asking them.

"Would the Croxsons do, then?" Nan queried timidly, often feeling more or less subdued by Harry's "goosie."

"The very thing," replied Rex; "they're so queer-looking, they'll make a jolly funny group."

"Shall I go for them while you're getting your *camera* ready?" remarked Harry, airing his knowledge of the photographic terms. Regie nodded yes, and Harry was off.

"Wouldn't it be nice to take them in that?" said Nan, pointing to one of the fishermen's boats drawn up upon the beach.

"Of course it would. You're splendid for thinking of things, Nan," Regie replied, proceeding to get his instrument in order. Nan helped him as best she could, very happy over the fact that such an important personage as he was considered her *splendid* for anything.

Meanwhile the Croxsons were hurrying into a miscellaneous assortment of threadbare out-of-door wraps, which were supposed to keep the cold out, but in point of fact did nothing of the sort. They were highly elated over the prospect of having their photographs taken. Not one of them had ever experienced that sensation before.

"W-w-won't it be a lark to be t-t-took?" stuttered little Madge, beside herself with excitement; and the flushed faces of the other four children showed that they undoubtedly thought it would, the neglected little quintette never dreaming that they had been invited because they were so "queer looking" and would make "a jolly funny group." But if Regie and Harry and Nan did sometimes have a little fun at the Croxsons' expense, they were too well-behaved ever to let them have an inkling of it. As for Regie, he was as gallant in his manner to these shabby little specimens as to the would-be little aristocrats in velvet knickerbockers and patent leather pumps whom he was accustomed to meet at dancing school. When the Croxsons arrived on the scene, Regie, having succeeded in fastening his camera to the tripod, had just plunged his head under the black rubber cloth which hung over it.

"What are you doing?" Joe Croxson made so bold as to ask.

"Focussing on the boat," was Regie's mysterious reply, from the folds of the rubber cloth.

At this answer Madge seemed to be somewhat intimidated. The word focussing had an ominous sound in her ears.

"What do you mean by that?" Joe asked gruffly, for not one of the little party was a whit wiser than before.

"Oh, I'm fixing things so as to be able to take a clear picture of that boat," Regie answered, good-naturedly; "and now I would like you all to run and get into it, ready to be taken."

At this the party would have scampered off to do his bidding but for little Millie Croxson, the baby, who had succumbed to a nameless fear, and had to be coaxed and carried to the scene of action. Regie stood at a little distance, wondering how he should pose his party, when suddenly Nan exclaimed, "Oh, I say! let's do this; let's pretend we have been shipwrecked, and had to take to the boats, and are out on the open sea. And you might take two pictures, Rex, one where we think we must all die in the boat, and

Said Nan, "let's pretend that we've been shipwrecked, and had to take to the boats, and are out on the open sea."

one where we have hailed a steamer, and are going to be picked up and saved."

Certainly Nan *was* splendid for thinking of things, and the children took to the idea at once; but it took somewhat longer to arrange matters to the satisfaction of everybody. Finally it was arranged that the four girls should be huddled together in the stern of the boat, and Joe and Jim Croxson should each have an oar, and lean way forward, as though they were rowing against a very heavy sea, and that Harry should be stationed on the bow as a look-out. Harry and Nan endeavoured, by turning their coats inside out, and one or two other alterations in costume, to make themselves as forlorn as possible. There was something pathetic in the fact that even the Croxsons themselves realised they need attempt nothing in this direction; they were sufficiently forlorn as they were.

Little Millie was supposed to be a half-starved little baby, and had an old handkerchief tied three-cornerwise about her head. As she sat on Nan's lap her thin little face looked the character to perfection.

"Now," said Rex, when all was in readiness; "you mustn't move, not one of you."

"C-c-can we w-w-wink?" stuttered Madge.

"Are we forlorn enough and sorrowful enough?" asked Nan.

"How do I look?" urged Harry, who stood balanced on the look-out in the stiffest of positions.

"Oh, you are all right," Regie answered, collectively; "now, still, every one of you."

Trembling with excitement he uncapped the lens, while he counted one, *two*, three, *four*, which were supposed to cover two seconds in time; and then pop! on went the cap again, but alas! the picture was not taken. Rex had forgotten to draw out the slide which would let the picture in on the plate; but before he had time to announce his discovery the children had abandoned their positions in the boat, and were crowding once again around the camera.

Regie hated to acknowledge his carelessness. He was loth to

take a single step down from the pinnacle on which the children had placed him because of his acquaintance with the photographing art, but it had to be done.

"You'll all have to go back and be taken over again," he said, disconsolately. "I didn't get any picture that time, because I forgot to do something I ought to."

The children marched back to the boat, but with faith evidently weakened in the real ability of this would-be photographer. It took some time to gain the properly forlorn expression and look of general despondency, but at last all was in readiness, and the picture was taken.

"Now change your positions and smile like everything," called Rex, "as though you saw the steamer that is going to rescue you coming toward you, and I'll take the other picture in a jiffy."

The children brisked up and obeyed Regie's orders by grinning from ear to ear, with the exception of baby Millie, whom neither petting nor teasing could coax into so much as the suggestion of a smile. This having your picture taken still seemed to her an uncanny and perilous proceeding.

"Say, Rex!" called Nan, in an anxious tone, "the baby won't look cheerful. I can't make her smile, no matter what I do."

Here was a real difficulty! Rex walked over to the boat to give the matter his personal attention.

"Perhaps it's too young a baby to understand that she isn't going to be drowned," suggested Madge, who was really quite experienced in the matter of babies, having had almost entire charge of Millie from her birth.

"Why, of course she is," Nan replied, blaming herself for not having thought of this way of solving the problem; "she's hungry and cold still, and she shouldn't smile."

So little Miss Millie's downheartedness proved no obstacle after all, and Regie soon announced that picture number two was taken. Pell mell the children scrambled out of the boat and hurried back to the camera.

"Let's see it, Rex." "Is it good?" "Which is the best?" were their exclamations all at once.

"Why, I can't tell you yet," answered Regie, out of patience with such ignorance; "don't you know I have to take the plates home before you can tell a thing about them, and develop them?"

"Develop?" said Jim Croxson, not having the remotest idea what the word might mean; "develop your grandmother! It's my opinion if a fellow had taken a picture he'd be glad enough to show it. I don't believe you can take 'em at all, and there's no use in wasting any more time in this tomfoolery. Come, Croxsies, let's travel home and scare up something to eat."

Jim was a ringleader in that family circle, and the younger

Croxsons took their departure with sullen faces, which looked as though they had spent more time in the weary activity of *scaring up* something to eat, than in the more passive and beneficial process of eating. Regie stood looking after them.

"I call that pretty mean," he said, angrily, "and it shows just how much they know about it."

"Mean!" muttered Nan, with her little lips pressed tightly together; "I would just like to see that Jim Croxson come up with."

Nan did not know exactly what was involved in this proceeding of being "come up with," but she had an idea that it was just about the most dreadful thing that could happen to anybody. Harry stood non-committal. Of course he thought it was very foolish for the Croxsons to go off like that; but he would himself see the thing through before expressing an opinion. If Regie said something more was needing to be done, he supposed he must believe him; but it certainly seemed, if a picture was taken, it was taken, and he ought to be able to show something for it.

"Say, Harry," asked Regie, as they walked home, "isn't there a big dark closet up in the attic?"

"Yes, as dark as Egypt."

"Well, then, we'll go up there to develop the pictures. I'd like to have you and Nan see me do it. Is the closet large enough for three?"

"Plenty."

"All right then; and will you carry up a bucket of fresh clear water, while Nan helps me to get my bottles and trays together?"

Harry's faith began to revive. "Rex does seem to know what he's about, after all," he thought.

Coats and hats were punched on to their respective pegs, rather than hung up according to rule, and in a few moments Harry, with the bucket of water, and Rex and Nan, with their mysterious vials and bottles, met in the dark closet. Rex lit his ruby lantern, and then solemnly closed the door. Poor little Millie would undoubtedly have been frightened to death had she been compelled to be present at this gloomy stage of proceedings.

Harry and Nan sat on the floor, with their legs crossed under them, tailor-fashion, and with their heads pushed very forward so as not to miss anything. Regie sat opposite them, pouring liquids out of bottles, measuring them in little glasses, adding water to them, and emptying them again into certain square trays, or dishes, in front of him.

"Now we're ready to begin," he said at last, with the air of a little lecturer; "and the first thing to be done is to take the plate out of the holder. This is the one on which I took the first picture; but you see it looks perfectly white, as though there were no picture at all."

"And is there?" asked Nan, incredulously.

"Of course there is, and you'll see it with your own eyes in a minute. First, I have to dust it with this camel's hair brush, for the smallest speck would make a little pin hole in the plate; and now watch! I put it in this tray; the stuff in here is called the developer, because in a few moments it will begin to bring the picture out."

This was always a moment of supreme excitement for Regie. You could have heard him panting away through the crack of the closed door. The excitement was contagious, and Nan began to pant too. Only Harry continued to breathe quite regularly.

"There it comes, there it comes!" Regie cried exultingly. "There's the boat, see! and there you are, Nan, and there! the Croxsons are coming out;" this in a regretful sort of tone, as though he half repented having included such a disagreeable crowd in the picture at all.

Mute with wonder, Harry and Nan looked on. To accomplish such a result in such a mysterious way raised Regie in their eyes to the level of an actual magician. Yes, there was the whole picture before them. They could distinguish it quite distinctly, even by the dim lantern light, only everything was reversed; faces were black and coats were white.

"That is the reason they call this a negative," Rex explained; "I think it means, not what it ought to be, because when this plate is dry, and we lay a piece of sensitised paper against it and put it in the sun, the print that comes off on the paper is called a positive; that is, we have a proof, a picture, as it ought to be."

"What do you do now?" asked Nan, in an awed whisper.

"Why, now I take it out of the developer and plunge it up and down several times in this bucket of water, to wash the developer off, and now I put it in this other tray; there's a solution of soda in here."

"Solution of soda?" thought Harry. "Dear me! Regie does know a lot for a boy of his age."

"What does the soda do?" he asked.

"It eats something off the plate, I think," Regie answered,

somewhat vaguely; "something I believe that ought to come off. And now I wash it thoroughly again, and now I put it in this third tray, which has a solution of alum in it. The alum gives the plate a good colour. Now another good washing and it is finished."

All this required much more time than it takes to write about it.

"As soon as the plate dries we can print a proof from it," Rex farther explained, "that is, if the sun stays out. Would you like to see me do the other one?"

"*Like* to see you!" said Nan, in a tone as though she wondered if Regie could possibly think for one moment that anything could at all compare with just this very thing that they were doing.

XIX.

Holidays in Town.

IN the summer weather all Moorlow, and indeed all the dwellers along the whole length of the shore, would gather in little groups on the beach to see the moon rise; but to-night the moon and the waves have the beach to themselves, for the ice is several inches thick on the fresh water ponds, and the wind is keen and biting.

Straight out of the ocean, with no summer fog to veil her coming, rises the great golden moon, and soon she is high enough to send a broad path of light shimmering across the water. And now she lights the way for Captain Murray's man Joe, trudging home from the village with the mail; and now she peers in through the dimity curtains of Nan's pretty room, making it bright as the day.

And what does she find there but something that never was there before; a bran new little trunk, with N.M. in black letters on the end toward the window, and no doubt she wonders if it can be possible that Nan is going away; little Nan, who never remembers having slept a night of her life out of sound of the sea. Travel on, old Moon, over the roof, until you can shine in at Sister Julia's window, and there you will discover two other trunks, which are ready for a start on the morrow, for *you* should know what every one else already knows—that Rex is going home, and Harry and Nan go with him to make a visit. Did you not discover as you sailed over the ocean the good ship *Alaska* drawing nearer and nearer, with Regie's papa and mamma on board? And do you not think, with your clear light to aid her, she will surely reach port by day after to-morrow?

But while we are so foolish as to stand out here in the cold, talking at the moon, Joe has reached the house and gone in with the mail, and among the other letters is a neat little package for Regie.

"Oh, here are the photographs!" he exclaimed; and right away there is such a solid little group, bending closely about him, that if it were not for the difference in the colour of hair you could hardly have told where one head commenced and the other ended. The children had been looking anxiously for these photographs for a week.

When Regie found from the proofs that the pictures that he had taken were satisfactory, he sent the plates up to New York, by express, to a photographer, who was accustomed to print his pictures for him, but he had heard nothing from them, and began to think they had gone astray.

It would have done your heart good to have heard Captain Murray's laugh as he looked at them. The one where the steamer was supposed to be coming to the relief of the shipwrecked mariners was, if possible, the funnier of the two. Nan was the only one who had fully entered into the spirit of the thing, and really looked as though something joyful was about to appear. The others had smiled, as they were bid, but a heartless conventional smile is at the best a sorry affair, and doubly so on such pinched little faces as the Croxsons'.

But the pictures, as pictures, were good, and Rex had no need to be ashamed of his work. He imagined he could see Papa Fairfax now, and how much amused he would be by them.

As this was to be the last of the many happy evenings they had spent together in the little cottage, it occurred to Sister Julia that it ought to be celebrated in some special way, so she crossed the room and whispered to Mrs. Murray. As the result of the whispering Mrs. Murray asked the children "what they would say to a candy-pull." Much scurrying about on the part of the children, and the delicious odour of boiling New Orleans molasses, which presently pervaded the house, showed they had said "yes" to the suggestion, and in the heartiest fashion possible.

At eleven o'clock, after enjoying to the full all the fun and satisfaction attending a thoroughly successful candy-pull, his little Royal Highness and the body-guard retired to rest, or, in less kingly English, Rex, Harry, and Nan tumbled into bed; and indeed it was high time, if they were to be ready for an early start in the morning.

To Nan and Harry Mr. Fairfax's house in town was a revelation. They were fortunate enough to be blessed with a comfortable and pretty little home of their own; but here was a home that was vastly more than comfortable and pretty. Nan gave vent to her admiration in a succession of audible "ohs!" the moment they entered the house, much to the amusement of Mrs. Mallory, the old housekeeper, who was glad enough to welcome them into the house that had been "such a lonely place without Rex and Mr. and Mrs."

"You like it, don't you, Nan?" said Regie, beaming proudly.

"It is perfectly beautiful," Nan answered, sinking down into a great easy chair, and trying to look everywhere at once. She was not in the least overpowered by the new surroundings, only supremely delighted.

"And to think we are to stay a week!" she exclaimed, with a happy sigh.

Harry, of a more enquiring turn of mind, was walking about the parlour, gazing up at the pictures, and making so bold as to touch certain little ornaments and articles of bric-a-brac to see how they felt.

When Mrs. Mallory had helped the children to lay off their

wraps, she showed Harry and Nan all through the house, taking as much pleasure in their exclamations of wonder and delight as though she herself owned everything in it.

Two members of the party from Moorlow did not seem in the least overjoyed at their arrival at the house in town. Secured by one leash, Hereward and Ned followed Regie obediently enough, for they were too well trained to offer any resistance; but if you could have had a word with either of the poor fellows they would have told you that life at Moorlow was glorious freedom, and life in New York a sadly limited affair, with whole days together when they did not have so much as a run in the park. So it was not strange that they suffered themselves to be led down the kitchen stairs, and out to their kennels in the little city yard, without one sign of jubilance over their return. If Mr. Fairfax had been on hand to welcome them, no doubt there would have been no end of boisterous demonstration, for the joy of seeing their master would have eclipsed the thought of how changed their life was to be. Early the next morning a telegram from their friend at the Highland Light came, addressed to Regie, and announced that the *Alaska* had been sighted from Sandy Hook, and would reach her pier about half-past eight. Then there was such a hurry and flurry, for the telegram had not been delivered very promptly, and there was no time to spare. Mrs. Mallory went flying bare-headed round the corner to order a carriage from the livery stable, while Sister Julia and the children ate a hasty breakfast.

"Drive as fast as possible, please," said Sister Julia, bundling the children into the carriage, and she reached up and dropped something into the driver's hand; the only thing, in fact, that ever seems to impart any real life to a livery team of horses.

They reached the pier just in time, for the *Alaska* was so near you could almost recognise anyone on board. Realising that they must not lose a moment, Sister Julia, with the children following close after her, pushed her way as politely as she could through the crowd. Indeed, people rather made way for them, for there was that in their eager, childish faces which seemed to make everyone feel that they must not be disappointed in the matter they had in hand.

As soon as they succeeded in reaching the edge of the wharf, Regie discovered Papa and Mamma Fairfax, close to the rail, in the very bow of the steamer, and his enthusiasm found vent in a lusty hurrah at the top of his lungs, to the general amusement of everyone.

Somehow or other they all managed going home to crowd into the same carriage, notwithstanding the wraps and portmanteaus, and then such a laughing, chattering party as they were! People on the side walk, and people in the street cars, could not keep from smiling as they glanced in at the noisy, merry load.

There is no gladness surpassing that of a happy home-coming, after a long and distant journey, and it is sad that we so soon settle back into the old routine of life and forget how supremely happy we were.

Fortunately for the Fairfax household, just this sort of gladness lasted for a whole week. Papa Fairfax went but once to the office, and Mamma Fairfax unpacked little beside the Christmas presents. In whole-souled fashion they simply gave themselves up to the amusement of the children.

Christmas came midway in the week, and such a Christmas! Nan may live to be ninety, but she'll never forget it, and Harry may grow to be a man with all sorts of cares and responsibilities, but he'll never forget it. Indeed, these two little people had so many treasures thrust upon them, that Mr. Fairfax thought best to make them a present of an extra trunk, in which to carry home their booty.

"All hands" were constantly on the go—morning, noon, and night I was going to say, for each day Mr. Fairfax planned some fine sight-seeing scheme, and every afternoon they "topped off" with an invigorating sleigh ride.

It was an ideal Christmas week, with a heavy fall of snow preceding it, and clear, cold weather that kept the sleighing in perfect condition until its close, and for many days after.

There was not a prettier turn out in the park than Mr.

Fairfax's Russian sleigh with its red plumes and black horses, and many a one turned and gazed at the merry load as it passed.

"That's the foinest paarty what sleigh-roides in this park," said a burly Irishman to one of his brother policemen, as they jingled merrily by on the day after Christmas; and, for one, I think he was quite right in the matter.

Mrs. Fairfax and Harry and Regie were on the back seat enveloped in a great white bearskin robe. It was Nan's turn to ride in front with Mr. Fairfax, and there she sat, a charming embodiment of serene satisfaction. I think even Mrs. Murray would hardly have recognised her own little Nan in an otter-trimmed dark-red coat, with an otter cap and muff to match. Mrs. Fairfax had bought the pretty outfit for her in Paris, and it was wonderfully becoming. Indeed, I believe there was a touch of pride in her bright little smile this morning, but I guess we can forgive it, if the head of this little Moorlow maiden was a trifle turned by the joyous experience of a happy week in New York at the gayest time of the year. Remember, too, that she had been the owner of this beautiful coat scarcely twenty-four hours, and I think you will admit

her to be made of different stuff from other little maidens did she not feel considerably elated by it. But Nan is not vain by nature, and never you fear but that she will go back to Moorlow the same dear child that she left it.

At the upper end of the park Mr. Fairfax met two old bachelor friends driving in a low cutter, whereupon the whole sleigh-full favoured them with the most smiling and cordial of bows. Harry and Regie were too fond of the accomplishment of gallantly touching their hats to lose a single opportunity, and Nan "was not going to sit stiff and straight as though she did not know anybody."

"Fairfax seems to get more out of life than any fellow I know," remarked one of the old bachelors; "and he's a good sight better-looking than he used to be. I wonder how it is?"

"Well, I'll tell you how it is," answered the other; "he's a deal happier than he used to be. They say his wife's a real treasure. I suppose that sort of thing goes a long way toward making a fellow get a good deal out of life. Then Fairfax has told me himself how much they enjoy that boy of theirs, and they ought to. It was a mighty kind thing to do. You know they did not have any children of their own, so they adopted that youngster of Will Reginald's."

"Yes, I know," replied Bachelor No. 1.; "but who are the other two children?"

"Why, I heard at the club last night that they are a pair of French orphans that they picked up in Paris. They have just returned from abroad, you know. I wonder where they'll stop; they seem to have a passion for adopting."

Surely the merry party in the Russian sleigh would have laughed harder than ever could they have heard all this.

A pair of French orphans indeed! Nan and Harry Murray; whose every look and accent betrayed them such thoroughgoing little Americans, and for whose home-coming a father and mother were waiting so impatiently. But that's about as straight as the world often gets things.

XX.

In Mr Vales Church.

S soon as Mr. and Mrs. Fairfax returned Sister Julia went back to her work at the great hospital. Mrs. Fairfax begged her to stay through the holidays, and the children coaxed and coaxed, but to no avail, for she knew that "little lame Madeline," as every one called her, was longing for her to come. Madeline had been in the hospital once before, and for almost a year, but now she had come back to stay. The doctors said she would never be able to leave it again, nor would she be there very long. The best of care and kindest of nursing must soon fail to cage the little spirit in any house that human hands had made.

"I can understand how you feel that you must go," Mrs. Fairfax had said to Sister Julia at the close of a long talk they had been having about it; "but it does seem too bad that you should take up your hospital work again without having had a vacation."

"Vacation!" laughed Sister Julia. "Why, I have just come home from the happiest vacation of my life!"

"But you were at work all the time caring for Reginald, teaching the children, and, hardest of all, tending those poor wrecked sailors."

"Yes, but it was all a pleasure. Every day I was breathing that strong salt air, and taking long strolls on the beach. To have chosen your life work, and to feel yourself hour by hour gaining strength and health that enables you to keep cheerily and

steadily at it, why, there is no happiness for me, Mrs. Fairfax, that at all compares with that; and while that state of things continues, no idle vacation, if you please. I should be half miserable all the time."

Mrs. Fairfax knew that Sister Julia was right in the matter, and bade her good-bye and God-speed with tears in her eyes, but they were tears of loving appreciation, and not because she did not expect to see Sister Julia soon again. Indeed, it had been arranged that she should come down from the hospital the very next Sunday, and go with the children to the afternoon service at Mr. Vale's church.

Sunday came—a clear, cold Sunday, and little Nan woke and gave a sigh as she looked about the little room that had been hers for a week. It was a beautiful room. She was lying in the shiniest of little brass bedsteads, and there were lovely pictures on the walls, and pretty things of one sort or another on every side.

"Dear me!" she thought, a little regretfully; "only one more night, and we must go home," but at the same time that one word *home* sent a glad little thrill through her heart. She felt sure that, after all, she would not exchange her own little room, with its wide-reaching view skyward, and landward, and seaward, for the finest room in the city, overlooking only a narrow street, and dreary stone walls and pavements; besides, though everyone had been so kind, and she loved them all dearly, it would be nice to curl up in her own mother's arms again, for even an eight-year-old little woman sometimes clings tenderly to certain comforts and luxuries of babyhood.

Sister Julia came at a quarter of four, and found the children eagerly waiting for her. As they walked down Fifth Avenue people looked with considerable interest at the sweet-faced woman, whose dress betrayed her a member of a sisterhood, and at the three children, who kept up a constant exchange of the place of honour, which consisted in being close to Sister Julia, on one side or the other, where they could have the privilege of clasping whichever hand was in best condition to forego the comfort of her muff.

There was nothing connected with this visit to which Nan and Harry had looked forward with more pleasure than to seeing Mr. Vale's church, and hearing him preach; and with beaming faces they followed Rex to the pew which they were to have quite to themselves, for Mr. and Mrs. Fairfax had gone to spend the afternoon with Grandma Fairfax, in Brooklyn.

"I think the church is beautiful," whispered Nan to Sister Julia.

"I knew you would like it," Sister Julia whispered back.

"The stained-glass windows are lovely, with the light coming through them."

"Yes," answered Sister Julia, for she did not fancy prolonged conversations in church.

"Must have cost a lot," Harry remarked to Regie, after staring all about him, and turning his body from side to side, in a take-everything-in sort of fashion.

"Yes, it did," Regie replied; "Mr. Vale thought the rich men ought to make it as beautiful as their homes."

"Who do you have to blow your organ, a man or a boy?"

"It's run by water-power, you goosie."

"What do you mean by that?" Harry asked, with knitted eyebrows.

"I would rather you would not talk any more now," Sister Julia interrupted, for she could see that the children's stage whispers were audible several pews away.

They were quite willing to be silent, however, for Mr. Vale had come into the chancel, and they felt themselves on their good behaviour; beside, they were too much interested in his every gesture to have eyes or ears for aught else. Indeed, Nan was by nature a most devout little worshipper. She loved everything connected with the service. Long before she knew one letter from another she had her own little prayerbook in the chapel at Moorlow, and would turn from page to page, as though perfectly familiar with the order, and during the responses she would emit certain audible little sounds, which greatly amused other children near her, and yet, to her little ladyship, were perfectly satisfactory. But she entered even more heartily into this afternoon's service than ever before.

Mr. Vale's earnest spirit seemed always to pervade the whole congregation worshipping in the old Tower Church. They knew he never preached a word which he did not faithfully strive to practise, and even little folk feel the power of a consistent life, before ever they can tell what the power is or why they feel it. There was much in this afternoon's sermon that the children could understand, and only once was Nan's attention distracted; that was when a restless little five-year-old, who sat before them, having disappeared for several seconds in the bottom of the pew, suddenly popped up again, dangling her button-boots and stockings over the back of the seat.

Harry and Rex clapped their hands over their mouths to keep from laughing outright. Nan smiled, and touched Sister

Julia, who leaned forward and succeeded in inducing her to quietly put them on again. That was the first the little witch's father knew of the transaction, for he had been listening intently to the sermon; but he looked gratefully at Sister Julia when he saw what she had done, and shook his head, as much as to say, "She is a most unruly little maiden."

After this performance the child leaned her head against the back of the pew, and became absorbed in a study of the stained-glass window over the chancel. No wonder it attracted her childish gaze. At the beginning of the service the light had fallen upon it from without, but now the wintry twilight was gathering fast, and the rims of brass in which the discs of glass were set were brilliantly flashing from the glow of the gas-jets. Ere long the service is over, and people are leaving the church. Reluctant to go, the children linger a moment in the pew, and fortunately too, for Ole, the old Norwegian sexton, is elbowing his way toward them, with a message from Mr. Vale. Quite out of breath he reaches them, explaining that "Mr. Vale would like to have the children come up to the study, and that he said he would see them safely home if Sister Julia must hurry back to the hospital."

Harry and Nan give Sister Julia a good-bye hug, "real hard," for they will not see her again before going home to Moorlow to-morrow; and then with happy hearts they follow Ole up the winding stairs that lead to the study.

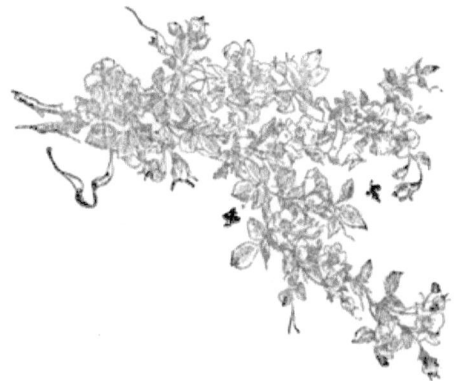

XXI.

In Mr Vale's Study.

MR. VALE was waiting for the children, holding the study door wide open to light them up the stairway.

"Come right in," he said; "I am proud to have my first visit from my little Moorlow friends;" then turning to the sexton, he added, "We may be here for some time, Ole, and if you wait for us, it will make you late for your supper, so bring me the keys of the church when you are ready to go, and I'll take them home with me to-night."

Ole, looking grateful for this thoughtful suggestion, trudged downstairs again, and the children walked into the room. Regie had been there several times before, but even to him it never looked so cosy as to-night. There was a bright fire on the hearth; Ole had been watching and stirring it up, for Mr. Vale had told him he expected to entertain some little folks after service. A cheery lamp was lit on the study table, as by this time it was quite dark out of doors, and near it some loving member of the congregation had placed a vase full of beautiful roses. On one side of the room were tall book-cases, reaching to the ceiling, and on the other three sides hung quaint old-fashioned portraits of some of the former rectors of the parish.

As soon as Nan heard Mr. Vale tell Ole that they would probably be there for some time, she quietly walked over to one corner, took off her hat and cloak, and carefully and smoothly laid them across a chair.

"Why, Nan child, who asked you to take off your things?" exclaimed Harry.

"Mr. Vale said we were to stay some time," Nan replied, not at all disturbed; "and I think it seems cosier to take off your things."

"I quite agree with you," said Mr. Vale, heartily; "and these young gentlemen cannot do better than to follow your example, for we are going to draw up to the fire and have a good talk."

So Harry and Regie, nothing loath, slipped out of their overcoats, and the little party gathered about the fire, the boys seated on either side of Mr. Vale's easy chair and Nan on his knee.

"Well, what did you think of the service?" he asked, taking Nan's little hand in his. "I know you could not have enjoyed it as much as I enjoyed looking into the upturned faces of my little Moorlow friends. It seemed as though you sort of belonged to my congregation, and ought to be there always.

"I wish we could," sighed Nan, shaking her head thoughtfully. "I knew all the time you must be a lovely preacher, and really I think you are the nicest minister there is."

"Why, so does everybody with any sense that ever heard him," said Regie, and in a tone as though there could not be the slightest doubt on that question.

"Oh, Rex! you are a good friend of mine," laughed Mr. Vale, affectionately, laying his hand over on Regie's knee.

"You love children, don't you, Mr. Vale?" remarked Harry, demurely, as though he had just made the discovery.

"Yes, indeed, Harry, and I hardly see how the old world could get along for a single day without them."

"I suppose you love 'em all alike, all the little children you know?" Nan said, rather regretfully.

"Do you think I ought to, Nan?"

"No, I guess not. I would like it better if you didn't; if you loved some of your little friends more than others."

"Why, what difference would it make to you?"

Nan hung her head and looked a little embarrassed.

"I think I know what she means," Harry said, slowly, who, by a glance toward Mr. Vale, had asked permission to turn the back log, and was at work with the tongs; "I think she means that she'd like to feel sure *she* was one of those you loved the most. Nan's kind of jealous sometimes."

"Well, I'm only jealous about nice things, any way, Harry Murray," and Nan sat bolt upright again; "I do not wish I had other boys' tops and marbles the way you do."

Harry was on the point of framing a quick retort, but he checked himself. He really was trying to be less of a tease, as far as Nan was concerned. Mr. Vale was the only one who noticed this little act of self-control.

"Good for you, Harry!" he exclaimed, "keep that sort of thing up, and I have no fears for the sort of man you'll make."

"Keep what sort of thing up?"

Regie and Nan looked at each other rather mystified, and Nan was very uncomfortable; besides, she did not enjoy the novel sensation of having had the last word, and she did wish Mr. Vale had not heard her speak that way to Harry. She wondered if he thought she was a regular little heathen.

"Keep what sort of thing up, Mr. Vale?" asked Regie, after a pause.

"Why, self-control, Rex. You see that remark of Nan's about tops and marbles made Harry feel like speaking back pretty sharply: so much like it that I fairly saw the words shaping themselves on his lips, but you did not hear them spoken, did you, Nan?"

"No," Nan confessed.

But if you had looked Harry's way just then you would have seen a queer little smile instead, which seemed to say, "Why, Nan's such a dear little thing I ought not to mind what she says."

"Well, that's just exactly what I was thinking," said Harry, astonished at Mr. Vale's power to read his thoughts.

"It was not very nice for me to tell that about the tops and marbles," Nan remarked, slowly.

"And it was not nice at all," said Harry, "for me to say that you were jealous sometimes."

"But I am," Nan truthfully admitted; "I know that well enough, only I do not like to be told about it."

"Of course you don't, Nan," and Mr. Vale drew the honest little maiden nearer to him. "Of course you don't, few of us like to be told of our faults; but we ought to like it, for often it would be the very best thing that could happen to us. Perhaps we should not go on making the same errors over and over again if somebody would tell us about them, and we could take the telling kindly."

"Mr. Vale," said Rex, who had been sitting thoughtful and silent for some time, "were you just a regular little boy?"

"Very irregular sometimes, I fear, only I don't quite know what you mean, Rex."

"Why, you see, I would like to be like you when I grow up; but I'm afraid I'm too different at the start. I mean did you use to be like other boys and me? Did you often get angry and speak back?"

"Yes, often; and in the sense that you mean I was indeed a regular boy; and do you think I never get angry now, Rex?"

"Perhaps you do now and then, but not often, I warrant, and when you do you keep it under."

"Keeping under is very hard work," sighed Nan, as though she had a world of experience in that direction.

"Keeping under is only another name for self-control, you know. And now, Nan," added Mr. Vale, "I am ready to answer your question, and to tell you that I do not love all the children I know alike by any manner of means. I love them in a dozen different ways. You see no thoughtful man grows to be as old as I am without wondering, whenever he looks into a little face, what sort of man or woman its owner will make. And so if I can I watch the little life closely, and after a while I see good traits and bad traits cropping out here and there, all in the veriest tangle; and by-and-bye, when I see the good traits growing faster and faster, I love that little life very hopefully and joyfully. Then suppose in another little life I see the evil things choking the good things, I love that little life very sadly and fearfully; or if I cannot make out which is getting the upper hand, I love it very anxiously; and so you see I do not love my little friends alike by any means. Now there you have had two sermons, one in the church, and one here in the study, and that is enough for one afternoon. Suppose you go to my table drawer, Nan, and see what you find."

Nan quickly slipped from his knee and pulled out the drawer.

"Three little boxes," she exclaimed, with delight.

"And what is written on them?"

How could she tell, this lazy little learner, who only lately had mastered plain printed letters? With a shy, half-apologetic look she placed them in Mr. Vale's hand.

"Regie, Harry, Nan," he read, handing each a box. Of course it was a present. With beaming faces they unwrapped them, and in each lay a square-edged, plain gold ring, with four old English C's engraved on the outside.

"One for each of us?" cried Nan, not knowing what else to say.

"Of course," said Mr. Vale; "I didn't see how I could make one ring do for three people, or I would, you know, for the sake of economy."

"And what are the C's for?"

"To help your growing up," Mr. Vale replied, and Nan looked a little mystified.

"Of course they stand for something," remarked Harry.

"Certainly, and for what do you think?"

"I shouldn't wonder if they stood for *control* every time," said Regie, with their recent conversation fresh in his mind.

"Not a bad idea," answered Mr. Vale, "and we'll let them stand for that altogether; but separately they are intended to stand for these four words, *Charitable, Cheerful, Courteous, Consistent.* Those are pretty big words for Nan, but I should not wonder if she understands them after a fashion."

"Yes," said Nan, with much dignity, for with the exception of the last word, *Consistent*, they all did convey to her a more or less definite meaning.

"I would like you to look up the exact definition of the words in the dictionary," added Mr. Vale, "and then I believe when you happen to look down on the four C's you will remember what they stand for, and that they will help you to build up the finest sort of a character. Now I propose that we do not tell anybody what those four C's stand for, keeping it for a little secret among ourselves."

"I would like just to tell Sister Julia," said Nan, "but, oh, dear me! I forgot I shall never see her again, perhaps."

"Why, of course you'll see her again," answered Regie; "don't you know that you and Harry are going to make me a visit every winter, and that I am coming to Moorlow for a while every summer? Why, I love every foot of the beach and the bluff from your house to the Life-saving Station."

"But, Mr. Vale, Regie can tell Sister Julia, can't he?" asked Nan; "she would love to know about them."

"Yes; and I think he might tell Papa and Mamma Fairfax, and Harry and Nan, Papa and Mamma Murray; but besides those five people I think it would be better not to tell anybody."

"So do I," said Regie, warmly; "if you told about them, other fellows might think you were setting yourself up to be sort of extra good, and they wouldn't understand."

"Exactly," Mr. Vale answered, "and so you see it will be wiser to keep the matter to ourselves, only I shall expect you to candidly report to me, once in a while, if you really are remembering to give those four adjectives a large place in your life."

"It was very, very kind of you to think of these pretty rings for a New Year present," said Nan, after a pause.

"And we're very much obliged, Mr. Vale," chimed in Harry and Regie; but the children's glowing faces showed deeper and more earnest thanks than could find their way into spoken words. Mr. Vale glanced toward the clock.

"I am afraid we must think about going," he said, "or they may think I have smothered you here in my study, like the poor little princes in the Tower."

"I wish we could stop in the church a moment and have a look at that organ," suggested Harry; "I never saw one that was run by water-power."

"We will then," answered Mr. Vale, "only hurry into your overcoats so that we shall not lose any time."

In a minute the little folk were ready, and each of the three gold rings was under cover of a warm silk mitten.

It was quite dark in the church, so that they took hold of

hands as they did that morning on the beach, and Mr. Vale led the way down the aisle to the choir-loft at the rear. When they reached the vestibule he went ahead and lit three or four burners, and the children followed him into a little room underneath the organ. Part of the machinery was here, and in a quick, clear manner, Mr. Vale explained its workings; then they went up into the choir itself to see the wonderful keyboard and pedals.

"Couldn't you play just one tune?" Nan asked, so beseechingly that Mr. Vale could not refuse the last request that he should probably hear for many a day from her little lips, so he whipped off his gloves and sat down on the high bench.

Mr. Vale loved nothing better than to play on that grand sweet organ, and to-night with those rapt little faces looking up to his he seemed fairly inspired. Without break or pause he glided from one sweet, solemn air to another, till suddenly realizing how late it was he began to play the German Evening Hymn, the one that Regie had sung at the Thanksgiving dinner at Moorlow. Regie took the hint, and straightway the sweet words rang out in his earnest, boyish voice, and so clearly, you could have heard each syllable in the farthest, darkest corner of the church. When he came to the verse—

> "Let my near and dear ones be
> Ever near and dear to Thee;
> Oh, bring me and all I love
> To Thy happy home above,"

he sang it with even a more intense earnestness, so that one could easily guess his thoughts.

Surely Harry and Nan were among Regie's "dear ones," and since they might not always be near to him, he threw his soul into the prayer, that they might always be near and dear to the Heavenly Father.

Another moment and the church was utterly dark again, there was the sound of the closing of a heavy door and the turning of a ponderous key in its lock; then all was still. Out in the wintry twilight four friends were walking homeward side by side, home through the frosty air; walking briskly, and yet with hearts a little heavy, for three happy months were at an end, and a little King and a faithful body-guard must part company on the morrow.

Printed by E. Nister at Nuremberg.

www.ingramcontent.com/pod-product-compliance
Lightning Source LLC
Chambersburg PA
CBHW020826190426
43197CB00037B/718